Helen Shipp

LET NONE DEAL
TREACHEROUSLY

D1416768

LET NONE DEAL TREACHEROUSLY

by Paige Cothren

Fulness House, Incorporated
Fort Worth, Texas

International Standard Book Number: 0-937778-03-6
© 1981 Fulness House, Incorporated
Published 1981. Second Printing 1983.
P. O. Box 79350, Fort Worth, TX 76179
Printed in the United States of America

DEDICATION

Let None Deal Treacherously was written with the memory of how I dealt treacherously against those who loved me most. This endeavor is humbly, gratefully, and tearfully dedicated to them, especially Foy, Fran, and Jay.

CONTENTS

FOREWORD

As a college and professional football player, Paige Cothren received numerous trophies and awards (All Southeast Conference, 1955-56; All South, 1955, 1956; three All American Teams, 1956; played in North-South Game, College All Star Game, Hula Bowl, Cotton Bowl, and Sugar Bowl; led Southeast Conference scoring and selected best blocker in Southeast Conference in 1955; held alone, or tied all national field goal records for season, game, and career; Los Angeles Rams and Philadelphia Eagles, 1957-59; kicked longest field goal for Rams and Eagles; led N.F.L. in field goals, 1958). He proved himself to be one of America's genuine all-star athletes. Today he is a remarkable trophy of God's grace. Paige is living proof of the transforming power of God's Word. The miracle only began with his dramatic conversion. Following his new birth experience at age 35, he gave himself continually to the reading of the Bible.

His hunger and thirst for fellowship in the Spirit, with Christ, through the Word became so insatiable at times that he would literally devour it for hours upon end without ceasing. The time he has spent alone with Truth has yielded fantastic results in his life. I can't overstate the importance of God's Word in the spiritual metamorphosis of Paige Cothren.

The mighty energizing power of God's Word within his life has turned a once-overbearing, egotistical, attention-seeking, pleasure-loving, ambitious, fearful, and frustrated athlete-businessman into a genuine Christian gentleman filled with the Spirit and saturated with the precepts of God.

It is exhilarating to witness the balanced lifestyle of this dear brother. He is a trim, healthy, physical man who gives honest, disciplined attention to his body, God's temple. He is a happy soul. His warm smile and iridescent countenance are evidences of his deep walk with our Heavenly Father. He advocates that strength of character comes only when we abide in Christ and adhere to the Spirit's admonition to ". . . put on the mind of Christ." Paige honestly seeks to have a servant's heart, and he has a sincere interest in the needs of others.

I am truly excited that Fulness House is publishing this much-needed book. All who read this valuable volume will surely be the richer for it. His candid openness in sharing intimate moments of struggle and conflict will often bring you to tears . . . and at times you'll "gasp" as he unravels shocking life-situations . . . and you'll laugh . . . get mad . . . rejoice . . . and marvel! I think also that you may return again and again to re-explore beautiful insights into real life revealed in these pages . . . and no doubt you'll find yourself quoting and referring to things he has said as you share with others.

Paige Cothren has seriously studied theology. His professional training has been extensive and of the highest caliber. In my opinion he surely has the gift of teaching. Like most genuinely honest men who have passed through the red-hot fires of heartbreak, violence, and "hitting the bottom," Paige determines to communicate healing truths to others and does so with great success.

As a counselor, he knows THE COUNSELOR. He continually meets people in one-on-one situations and it is glorious to know that many find hope in those sessions. The Word of God is his text for helping real people find real solutions to real problems.

I commend this book to you and the many others who will surely read it. As an evangelist I see many people come to Christ. Because of a lack of guidance and because of isolation from "solid spiritual food," many of them fail to grow up in Christ. What a tragedy! Oh to God that every convert would plunge as completely into God's Word as did Paige Cothren so soon after his conversion. Satan works overtime to prevent God's little children, the newborn, from getting into His Word. Without the Word there can be little growth.

I am delightfully enriched because my family and the Cothren family are friends. We share the blessed honor of being under the spiritual authority and God-anointed ministry of one of America's premier Bible expositors, our pastor, Dr. Bobby Moore. Paige's son, Jay, and my son, Van, played on the same high school football team. (Paige was their coach.) My wife, Sue, is Paige's secretary and she and Foy are dear sisters in Christ. Sue and I have been blessed to have observed firsthand as Paige and Foy have lived out their convictions. They are for REAL.

May this honest heart-throb of Paige Cothren be a tremendous joy and encouragement to you. After reading this fresh account of Christ's redemptive ministry "in the now," you will no doubt join me in praying that God will lead Paige to continue to share his ministry with us through the printed page.

Jerry Spencer, Evangelist
President, Global Outreach, Inc.
Memphis, Tennessee

PREFACE

On June 2, 1957, my fiancee', Foy Taylor, and I met at the altar of a little church in a small town in North Central Mississippi, an area known historically as a part of the (so-called) Bible Belt. There we became husband and wife—for fourteen years. In January of 1971 Foy Taylor Cothren appeared before a judge in the county courthouse. There, husband and wife, Paige and Foy Cothren, were proclaimed to be single! How did our marriage fail? Why did it fail? No one knew, not even us. Now, as Christians who believe the Bible, we know both how and why it failed. Praise God, His Word lays out perfectly the blueprint for marital success.

Foy and I have experienced both kinds of marriage: one of misery, ending in divorce; the other one in joy which God reconstructed around the Lordship of Jesus Christ. May this book enable you to embrace the latter.

INTRODUCTION

Originally, the primary purpose for writing *Let None Deal Treacherously* was to give counselees printed Biblical answers to their problems. Counseling would require less time, it seemed to me, if each counselee were able to take printed answers home to study. In vain I had searched for one book which covered the preponderence of counselees' problems. Thus, this book was not written to sell. However, through certain people and circumstances initiated by Sue Spencer, my secretary, I decided to investigate the possibility of having the manuscript published. Fulness House, Incorporated agreed to publish the book, for which I am very grateful.

The Flow of the Book

Let None Deal Treacherously consists of a series of eleven subjects loosely tied together, each a separate chapter. Because of the independence and distinctiveness of each subject, the book may not seem to flow smoothly from one chapter to another. Greater importance was assigned to the subject matter of each chapter than to smoothness of flow, therefore flow yielded to content.

Some counseling problems, family finances for example, aren't discussed. Included are the basic problems which appear in my counseling sessions most often. Usually financial situations and other problems have a way of changing when families begin to glorify the Savior in all areas of their lives.

The Title

The title, *Let None Deal Treacherously,* comes from the book of Malachi, chapter two. Before the Babylonian captivity, many Jewish husbands "put their wives away," or divorced them. Through Malachi, God's messenger, the Lord warned Jewish men to ". . . take heed to your spirit, and let none deal treacherously against the wife of his youth." (2:15) As in modern America, the caution went unheeded, and God judged the nation.

The Material

Much of the material which comprises this book may be different from that which you have heard before. Questions may emerge concerning the truthfulness and/or the workability of the examined concepts. I invite those questions while imploring you to accept no unscriptural teaching in the book. Likewise, please reject none of its truth. Using the Bible, test the teachings contained in the book. For an honest writer and teacher, joy comes from having his readers and students search the Scriptures to prove his material.

Guard Against Resistance

Because some of the concepts expressed in *Let None Deal Treacherously* might be new to you, you may experience an emotional and mental resistance to them. May I ask you to consider very carefully the material in the book and, as previously mentioned, either accept it or reject it as you weigh its truthfulness against the Scriptures.

Seminars

My wife Foy and I have taught and are continually teaching this information, not only in counseling sessions, but in marriage seminars, in churches and church retreats. Our Lord has used these concepts to change lives. We desire that God will change your life through them and, if needed, heal your marriage. Both will come, not by reading this book, but through your obedience to Him. The book should help you spot trouble and correct it. Correction means obedience to God.

Thank You

Several people have helped me complete *Let None Deal Treacherously*. My secretary, Sue Spencer, and Diane Maxwell, who is also a secretary at my church, have spent many hours typing, correcting, and retyping the manuscript.

When an editor of a publishing company suggested that I have someone write the Foreword, I immediately thought of Jerry Spencer, a much-traveled and God-used evangelist, and Sue's husband as well as a dear friend and brother in Christ. Jerry's remarks are very kind. Let me assure you that he is acutely aware that my life without Jesus amounts to nothing more than a "big pile of evil junk."

Thank you Sue, Diane, and Jerry. You are beloved sisters and brother in Jesus.

I

THE TALE OF TWO TESTIMONIES

A Danger

There is, of course, a tendency in the giving of a testimony for one to magnify the converted person rather than the Converter of the person. With all of my heart, allow me at the outset of this testimony to say, "I know better!" If in this writing, more importance seems to be placed upon Foy and me than upon our Lord and His work upon the Cross, please forgive me. I simply don't know how to deliver a testimony without overly using the condemning pronoun "I." I (you see?) confess to that extreme usage in the beginning of the story, casting myself upon your mercy, trusting you to understand. Foy and I live in full awareness of Whom we have believed. We know Who saved whom, and we have no desire, conscious nor subconscious, by His grace, to pull anyone's eyes from our Lord onto ourselves. So there; having thus proclaimed, permit me to continue.

My Childhood

My childhood was an unusual one to say the least. Given to me was the wonderful privilege of growing up in the rural South. In addition, I was reared in a home with my mother's three brothers, all of whom were college and professional football stars. Because my father, Wallace Cothren, "public worked" (as it was called then) in a distant town, as opposed to farming, my mother, Hilda, my sister, Wanda, and I lived with my grandmother, Mama Poole (Mrs. Emily Poole). Mama Poole's life is a story in itself and one that really bears telling. Time and space prohibiting that, allow me to tell you this. She lost her husband, Will Poole, to the then-dreaded disease, appendicitis, in the early 1930's. Mama Poole was left with a farmhouse, a 150-acre farm, and seven strapping children (four girls and three boys), the oldest boy, Buster, being thirteen years of age. With these children, a clear mind, hard physical work, and little else, the family survived through the hard years following the great depression. Mama Poole's life painted an almost perfect picture of the woman in Proverbs 31:10-31. What a "far cry" from the sensual, sexy, helpless picture of a female which Hollywood and New York have deposited in the minds of many Americans today, even professing Christians.

Two years before I was born in 1935, a coach at Ole Miss, the state university located in Northern Mississippi, heard about a big, hardnosed athlete who had just graduated from high school, Buster Poole. Coach Tad Smith boarded a train to Gloster in South Mississippi, the nearest town to Mama's farm. Getting directions in town, he caught a ride out to the farm, some ten miles away. Coach Tad found Buster cutting firewood behind the house and presented him with an athletic scholarship to Ole Miss. That unheralded and unpublicized event initiated a family tradition which would continue for many, many years. A great number of Pooles and relatives of the Pooles, like me, would play football for Ole Miss. From 1933 to 1978, more than fifteen Pooles, or those with Poole mothers, played football at Ole Miss. Five of us went on into professional football, gaining many honors both in college and professional ball. Four made All-American in college. Two made All-Pro. In 1942, there were five Pooles on the Ole Miss football team.

The College Years

Out of that background I appeared on the campus at Ole Miss in the fall of 1953. By then, Buster had completed his pro career with the New York Giants and had accepted an assistant coach's position at Ole Miss. Ray and Barney, his brothers, were still playing professional football, Ray with the Giants and Barney with Baltimore. By the fall of my sophomore year, I had been given the opportunity to become the starting fullback. That year, 1954, we won nine games and lost only one in the regular season. Navy, however, beat us rather soundly in the Sugar Bowl. Again in 1955, my junior year, we lost only one game, that one to Kentucky, in Lexington. The scoreboard loss wasn't my only one that night. I left some teeth on old Stoll Field, compliments of one Lou Michaels, who later became my teammate with the Los Angeles Rams. On New Year's Day, we beat Jim Swink and Texas Christian University in the Cotton Bowl.

I met Foy in the spring of my junior year at Ole Miss. We immediately began dating. Laughingly we tell, as a part of our testimonies, that Foy came to Ole Miss looking for a big football hero and I came looking for a rich Mississippi Delta coed. We found each other. Foy, although she wasn't from the Mississippi Delta, was the daughter of a very wealthy man, Mr. T. F. Taylor, Jr., from Eupora, Mississippi.

By the time the fall of my senior year rolled around, Foy and I were firmly "entrenched" with one another. In June, following a glorious college football career, Foy and I were married.

A Wedding—The First One

The church was packed for the wedding. All the newspapers in the area carried the story, not only in the society sections but also on the sports pages. By the day of the wedding I had been drafted and had signed a professional football contract with the Los Angeles Rams, and I had accepted an invitation to play in the 1957 College All Star Game at Soldiers Field in Chicago. What a story! What a wedding! It was the social event of that summer. Mr. Taylor had spared nothing in the wedding nor in the reception following it. How could a marriage which had such an exciting beginning fail?

Foy and I were both members of the same church denomination. There was no problem there. In fact the Bishop of the State of Mississippi performed the ceremony. Now, as a Christian preacher and counselor, looking back I suppose the most striking and alarming thing about our wedding ceremony is not what happened but what did not happen. Foy and I were never once asked the simple question, "Do you know Jesus Christ as your Lord and Savior?" Not only that, but no marriage counseling was done with either of us. We simply met at the altar in complete ignorance and blindness and were joined together in "holy" matrimony. There really wasn't much "holy" about it. Oh, to be sure, the ceremony was held in a church, but the location of a marriage ceremony doesn't make the marriage holy.

May I digress long enough to say this? As a preacher and counselor, I have come to the conclusion that I should not perform a wedding until I have spent at least three hours counseling with the bride and groom. The bride must spend one of her hours with my wife.

Anyway, Foy and I were married and after a short honeymoon I promptly left for six weeks of ROTC summer camp at Ft. Benning, Georgia. When that experience ended I went to Evanston, Illinois to play in the now-extinct College All Star Football Game against the New York Giants. Immediately after the game, which was played in Soldiers Field in Chicago, I flew to Los Angeles to begin living out a childhood dream, playing professional football. That the dream would actually come true was at that time far from being a certainty. I still had to make the club, no small endeavor. There were only twelve professional football teams in the country and each club could carry a total of only thirty-five players. What a challenge! What misery! Never knowing from day to day if I would be "cut," as being released from the club was called. I came to know the "Turk" intimately. He was the mythical character who would come "riding" through the training camp each morning wielding his mighty sword, cutting players from the team. Many hopeful athletes came to hate the words: "The Coach wants to see you in his office. Bring your playbook." Somehow I made it through that first training camp without being cut.

Los Angeles—Exciting

The two years I spent with the Rams were exciting years from a worldly perspective. We lived in Hollywood in the twilight days of its glory as the movie capitol of the world and often saw very famous actors and actresses. Yet with all of that I wasn't happy. My hope and purpose in life revolved around being able to play professional football. I reasoned that it was the highest calling of man. If a person was to be happy in life, pro football would certainly do it. As a result of my unhappiness Foy and I began to argue. At first we fought mostly over little things. Later the little things were blown up into big things and we fought over them. (There was a reason. We discovered it after we became Christians, and it will be discussed in Chapters Three and Four). Our lives really began to drift apart during the second year at Los Angeles.

After my second season with the Rams I entered the artillery and missile school at Ft. Sill, Oklahoma. I had received my commission in the Army Reserve upon graduation from Ole Miss and had been assigned to the artillery branch. Flunking math in college as soundly as I did, I couldn't figure why the army assigned me to the artillery and missile school. The classes were almost all math and trigonometry. I had never even taken trigonometry at Ole Miss. The army very generously assigned me to my six months active duty artillery school precisely during the period of time between my second and third seasons.

The artillery and missile school lasted twenty-one weeks. Having a poor math background, it was unbelievably difficult to maintain a passing average. Each afternoon, as soon as I got home from classes, I would begin studying. At midnight I would stop, having taken only a thirty minute break for supper. Foy and I were spending absolutely no time together. She saw me off at 6:00 A.M. when I left for the post and that night during the thirty minute supper break. Occasionally, we would spend some time together on Saturday or Sunday afternoon. A marriage counselor is not required in order to recognize the fallacy in that behavior. Our lives then really began to drift apart.

Matters were not helped much when just a week before getting out of the army and reporting to the Rams training camp, I injured my right knee. Being a field goal kicker, the injury, although not requiring surgery, was serious. Before the first week of training camp had ended, I decided to go back to Memphis, Tennessee, to a surgeon friend for treatment.

Philadelphia—The End

Treatment for the injured right knee demanded that I remain in the hospital in traction for several weeks. When finally I was released from the hospital, I learned that the Rams had placed me on waivers. I had told them I was not going to play football again. The Philadelphia Eagles "picked me up." A month later Foy and I were living at the Old Penn-Sherwood Hotel in Philadelphia, a few blocks from Franklin Field, where the Eagles played all their home games.

Life in the Penn-Sherwood was, to say the least, less than exciting. After living in the spacious apartment complex of Los Angeles, the tiny two-room apartment in which we found ourselves was depressing. The arguing and fighting between Foy and me increased. Life grew more miserable for both of us.

Finally the season was over. The most exciting thing that had happened the entire season happened against my old team, the Rams. I kicked three field goals, one in the final sixteen seconds to win the game. Immediately following the game the Rams coach, Sid Gilman, was fired.

The Move Into Business

Foy and I bought a home in Jackson, Mississippi, after the football season that year. I went into the real estate and insurance business just in time for the economic recession of 1960. A discouraging year later, after the birth of our precious daughter, Fran, we moved to Foy's home, Eupora, Mississippi. I wrote the Eagles that I was retiring from football.

I didn't enter retirement enthusiastically. I wanted to go back to Philadelphia, but not especially because I enjoyed pro football. I "needed" the roar of the crowd. I had heard it for a long, long time. I wasn't certain I would "make it" without it. I didn't, although I know now that I wouldn't have "made it" with the roar of the crowd either.

In Eupora I went into the shopping center and grocery business. Because of Foy's credit at the banks, I was able to borrow large sums of money. It wasn't long before I owned a supermarket and had built a shopping center. Pro football had let me down. I was not happy, but that would soon change, I supposed. Even though pro football had not filled the void in my life, I knew that success in business would.

Foy, Fran, and I were living in the big house in Eupora when our son Jay was born. Foy's mother and father had moved to Ft. Lauderdale, Florida and had left the house to us. It was some home! Three stories, innumerable rooms, thick carpet, lavish furnishings. Later we put in a swimming pool and pool house, bar and all. That gave us two bars. We already had one in our den. By the world's standard, nothing was missing from my life. But something certainly was. I was more miserable than I had ever been.

I knew my trouble, I reasoned. I needed another supermarket. That would solve my problem. I wasn't cut out to own just one supermarket. I had executive potential! That's why I'm not happy, I concluded. At Ole Miss the rest of the student body had called football players "meatheads." That name always "stung" me just a little. That resentment probably helped motivate me to want to be an "executive." For whatever reason, that was what I wanted to be, an executive. I liked the sound of Paige Cothren, Executive, and I liked the thought of being one. I could practically see my name on my office door. So, with a close friend, I bought my second supermarket, in Fulton, Mississippi, some ninety miles north of Eupora.

With the purchase of that store so far away, I now had an excuse to stay out late at night. Occasionally I would stay gone all night. I told Foy it was business. After all, an executive on his way to the top of the grocery business could not be hampered by a little thing like coming home at night. Arguing, animosity, and hatred characterized our home. Foy, Fran, and Jay, those precious people, suffered.

Shortly after purchasing the store in Fulton I opened a third one, in Calhoun City, Mississippi. Now I would really deserve the title, executive. Surely now satisfaction and happiness would be mine. I was wrong. The third supermarket just increased my problems. That meant that now I had "life-controlling" problems at home and in my businesses. I began to invest money into other ventures. Pressure mounted on all fronts, in every area of my life. Night clubs, whiskey, pills, and sin became a way of life for me. I was never satisfied to take Foy out alone to dinner or to a nightclub. I wanted other couples and activity around me all the time. Introspection became the real fear of my life.

Since becoming a Christian, I have recognized myself in many verses of Scripture, but one of the most sobering passages is found in Proverbs, 4:14-16: "Enter not into the path of the wicked, and go not in the way of evil men. Avoid it, pass not by it, turn from it, and pass away. *For they sleep not, except they have done mischief; and their sleep is taken away, unless they cause some to fall.*" (emphasis mine) The King James translation is kind to me. The word mischief means evil. My entire lifestyle was one of wickedness. I actually found no sleep unless I had been to a wild party and held plans for another on the next night. I wanted everyone to be engaged in immorality. To me, those repulsive people who walked into church with Bibles in their hands had not yet discovered the real meaning of life. Church was for the ignorant and unlearned. The contemporary, suave, sophisticated executive had moved on above and beyond church.

Something Missing

Realizing that something was drastically missing from my life, and being unable to discover it in business, money, family, nightclubs, whiskey, pills, and parties, I began to look elsewhere. I became the commanding officer in the local National Guard unit. I joined several local civic clubs. None of these things brought contentment. The single life! That was what was missing. I was not cut out to be married, I thought. Seemingly, it mattered little that I had a family. I reasoned that my children would be better off without me. After all, I was so unhappy I could not really be a father to them anyway. My choices seemed obvious enough. Stay married and be miserable; get a divorce and be happy. Little did I then know that divorce is not the answer either.

The Divorce

I did not even bother to go to the courthouse for the divorce trial. I let my lawyer do it. I was free, free again! Now I could do all the things which I had for fourteen years wanted to do, and without fear of being caught.

Before the date of the divorce, I had sold my stores in Calhoun City and Fulton. Disillusioned and unhappy with being an "executive," I really wanted to sell my Eupora store. About the time of the divorce, a friend asked me to take a position in a new company he had formed in Jackson, 120 miles south of Eupora. That made sense to me. I could keep my Eupora store. My mother and dad were managing it for me. Living out of town, I could escape the headaches involved in actually operating a store. I knew my parents would care for it as though it were their own. I would be earning a rather large salary in Jackson. I would be in a bigger town where no one could really keep up with what I was doing. There were many nightclubs, many women and many parties. I leased an apartment which opened up right onto a swimming pool and patio. I bought a new gold Corvette. I made plans to be a "playboy executive." I dated many women and there was one in particular whom I was planning to marry. I positioned myself for what I "knew" would be a life filled to the brim with "gusto" and pleasure.

I was miserable!

My misery permeated every part of my life. All the things upon which I had depended for motivation had failed me. Now the "ultimate" had failed. My freedom hadn't really been a freedom at all. Where does a person go when the "ultimate" in life only increases his misery?

I wanted to somehow start over. I wanted to "want my family again." I wanted to lose the desire for parties, drink, pills and all the rest. I wanted to be as I was when Foy and I first married.

On March 30th, 1971, I walked out of my apartment in Jackson, got into my gold Corvette and drove 120 miles to Eupora to talk to Foy. I'm honestly not certain what I expected to gain out of the conversation. I am certain that I went to gain, not give. My life was one of absolute selfishness. I was miserable so I offered to take my family back in order to be near someone who cared for me. My entire purpose for going back to Eupora that day was selfish.

Many men with whom I have counseled allow their lives to become so sin-ridden that they actually believe that it takes two worlds to sustain them. They want their family, but not their family alone. They also want that second world, the world of sin, momentary pleasure, and temporary freedom. With one hand, as it were, they grip the family. With the other hand they hold onto a life of sin. Holding onto both, they gradually sink into depression, struggling to keep their heads "above the water" of total hopelessness. They fear that the loss of either will plunge them into total purposelessness and take from them even their desire to live. Their struggle is one of survival. Almost every time, those who are obsessed with possessing two worlds will lose one of them. Sometimes, God will strip both away leaving them with no "lifeline" except Him. That is what happened to me.

When I arrived at Eupora that day Foy was cool but polite to me. I tested her, seeking to determine if I might come back. We were downstairs in the den when she told me that she had made plans for her life with someone else. Softly she told me it was too late for us.

I really don't remember everything that happened either before she told me that or afterward. I'm not even really certain that I had a great desire to get my family back. I am certain, though, that after she said what she did I realized that I had absolutely no reason in the world for which to live. I didn't want to live.

I'm not sure that I would have taken my life. To be able to truthfully write that would make the testimony much more dramatic, of course. I do remember that I wanted to die. Because I had whiskey and drugs in me there is a possibility I could have taken my life, I suppose. Fear and hopelessness gripped my heart at the thought of it. I started crying.

From Hopelessness to Hope

One of my best friends in the past had been my attorney, Rusty Denman. Rusty had worked for a while in Washington for a Congressman from the state of Mississippi. When the Congressman came back to Mississippi to run for Governor, Rusty came to Eupora and went into law practice. From the time he moved to town we had become friends. We jogged together. We partied together. We went on vacations together. We saw one another almost every day. But about two years prior to this day, something had happened to Rusty. Watching Billy Graham one night on television, Rusty gave his life to Jesus. Our paths just kind of parted. (I have discovered since becoming a Christian myself, that sort of thing happens). I really thought that he believed he was too good for me since he had "got religion." I didn't even want to associate with him.

Weeping hysterically at Foy's rejection, I called Rusty, not really knowing why. I sensed an overwhelming compulsion to talk to him. He said he could see me. I hurried into his office and immediately began to try to talk to him about all the things which were happening to me. But Rusty wouldn't talk to me about all of that. He wanted to talk about what he said was my real problem, my relationship to Jesus Christ. I remember trying to convince him that my life was at stake. I had no desire to live just five more minutes.

He answered by saying something like, "Paige, you need Jesus." I said, "Rusty, give me a reason to live; then I'll get things right with Jesus." I remember Rusty's next words and I believe I'll remember them even through eternity. Rusty looked across his desk at me. Speaking in a slow deliberate Southern drawl which is characteristic of both his nature and his profession, he said, "Paige, you've got it backwards. Give your life to Jesus and you'll have your reason to live.'

Rusty didn't understand, I thought. I wanted something valid, something concrete. Weeping bitterly, I made my way back outside to my car. Rusty followed me as I got into my car. He asked me to go with him to talk to someone. I asked, "Who?" He answered, "Stuart Angle. He's president of French Camp Academy."

I knew where French Camp was located. It is a small Mississippi village situated twenty miles south of Eupora on the Natchez Trace, a Federal Parkway. It also provided a place where I could stop and buy a 7-Up with which to mix my whiskey on my numerous trips from Jackson to Eupora and back.

I didn't really want to go to French Camp with Rusty. But thinking perhaps that someone there would listen to my story and, I suppose, perhaps sympathize with me, I went. Rusty had called Stuart and made an appointment for me to see him. That afternoon I walked into his office.

Stuart was different from most men whom I knew. I was accustomed to yelling and hollering. If, when I wanted to say something, someone else was talking, I just out-yelled him. My friends usually did the same. That was "standard operating procedure" for the kind of life which for years I had lived. Common courtesy had not graced my life. But when Stuart was talking and I interrupted, he would stop and listen to me. I remember thinking how unusual that was. Before long though, Stuart began to share Scripture and a little soul-winning tract with me.

For the very first time in my life, I cared about God's life-changing truths. I was a sinner. God had a plan for my life. My sins had separated me from God. That had thrust me from His plan for my life. Misery ensued. It all made sense for the first time. In Stuart Angle's office on the campus of that small Christian school tucked away inconspicuously in the hills of North Central Mississippi, God birthed me into His kingdom.

Later that night Rusty drove me back to Eupora, I knew I was saved. I knew by the grace of God the direction of my life from that moment. I had no "house" but I could with Joshua say, "But as for me . . .I will serve the Lord." The guilt was gone from my soul and I knew it.

As soon as Rusty and I arrived back in Eupora, I went to Foy's home. I knocked on the door. Foy came to the door, looked through a little glass window in the door and let me in. I was shocked somewhat that she had opened the door, for I had made two attempts on her life while we were separated. She was deathly afraid of me and had only let me come in earlier that afternoon because there was another adult present. She wouldn't allow me to come into the house at all after nightfall. In fact, her fear of me had partly motivated her to be courteous that afternoon. She had not wanted to do or say anything which might launch an emotional explosion. Foy knew I was capable of violence. But now, looking through the window, she saw a difference in my countenance. I wasn't aware that I appeared different. Foy later told me what made the difference. For the first time she saw no hate, no bitterness, no anguish in my face. I was at peace with God. The door opened.

"I'm Sorry"

"Foy, I'm so sorry." Those thoughts were ricocheting inside my brain as she opened the door. For the first time in my life I said, "I'm sorry." I was sorry; sorry for what I had done to my loyal wife and two precious children; sorry for the hurt I had caused my mother and dad; sorry for the embarrassment I had been to my faithful sister, Wanda; sorry for what I had done to Foy's mother and father (her father had passed away several years earlier); sorry for the filth I had brought into my community; sorry for my sins which propelled the Lord Jesus to the cross.

Foy and I talked that night. As the Lord Jesus is my witness, I'm not certain that the thought ever occured to me that I might get my family back. I wasn't even capable of verbalizing what had happened to me at French Camp. I knew I was saved but I didn't even know how to express it. I didn't know the language. I just knew that I wanted Foy to experience with the Lord what I had discovered that day. Even though she was a member in good standing of a local church, I knew she didn't have the kind of a relationship with God into which I had entered. We talked into the next day. Finally, after lunch Foy agreed to go to French Camp with me, the last request I would ever make of her. As inconceivable as it may seem, had Foy and I died that night, I would have gone to Heaven; she would have spent eternity in Hell.

We arrived in French Camp in the middle of the afternoon. From his office, Stuart invited us to go to his house. He and Foy went into his living room. I waited outside on the doorsteps. Fifteen minutes passed, then thirty; then an hour. At length, the door opened and Stuart invited me to come in. Foy had trusted her life into the worthy hands of the Lord Jesus Christ.

From hate to love; that was her journey that day. Because of all the things which I had done to her, Foy was filled with hate and bitterness toward me. But because of what Jesus had done for her, her hate was turned into love.

When Foy and I got back to Eupora, we sat down with Fran and Jay in an attempt to explain that no longer would they see what they had grown up seeing—fighting, cursing, drunken parties. Of course, they didn't comprehend all that was said. Jay was only eight years old, Fran only ten. They had never seen real love in either Foy or me. They weren't impressed by what we told them. We had said practically the same thing many times before, only to fail over and over again. This time, we avowed, things would be different because we had given our lives to Jesus.

A Family Reunited

I could write many books about the next few years of our lives. We viewed firsthand the power of God working in one another's lives. We experienced the healing effect of His Word as it purified our minds. We saw a family put back together.

Do you really believe that God exercises actual power in the physical lives of people today? To be classified as a "Bible believing" Christian, you will of course be forced to answer, "Yes." You may believe it intellectually. But do you REALLY believe it, I mean with the heart? Do you live your life depending upon that truth? That's the crux of real belief. It's the application of a life-changing truth, not just an intellectual assent to one.

Foy and I experienced the power of God as He changed us from the heart outward. We discovered the joy of a right relationship with Him. Love replaced hate for one another and for other people. A completely dead marriage came alive right before our eyes. When we began to live in obedience to God's Word, He began to bless us. He poured back into our hearts and minds all that was necessary for the marriage to work.

Foy and I had not had any kind of a relationship between us, physical, mental, or otherwise for years before the divorce. But now, as we yielded ourselves completely to Him, we were blessed with all that was essential for the marriage to be a good healthy one. There followed a miracle. Marital deadness burst into vibrant life.

God also allowed me to experience first hand the power of His Word. Many scars remained on my heart after salvation. I had hurt many people. Much of the guilt of those years of sin still lingered with me, although intellectually I knew that the sin had been forgiven and that the guilt was no longer mine to bear. Jesus had borne it on the cross. The old lifestyle born out of a life of sin no longer existed, but there were things and people for whom I still thought I cared. I hurt. Because I hurt, I spent time in God's textbook on hurt, the Bible. There, I soon discovered the great purifying and strengthening power of His Word. Jesus said in John 15:3, "Now you are clean through the word which I have spoken unto you." The word "clean" in the original language is the word from which we get the medical term "catheterize." The Word of God literally catheterizes our minds. That is, it drains away the impurities. What a precious discovery of truth! I found that when the memory of the guilt, hurt, and burden of the past began to depress me, and as I saturated my mind with God's Word, these things would just wane away. What a glorious weapon! As quickly as Satan plunged these memories into my mind, God's Spirit, working through His Word, would extricate them. I found myself suddenly hungering for His Word. Often I studied as many as eighteen hours a day, filling my mind with God's priceless truths. My sin-laden brain began to heal.

A Wedding—The Second One

On June 13, 1971, Foy and I were reunited at the same altar where in 1957 we had first been married. The wedding was attended by our pastor, who married us; Stuart and Ann Angle; Rusty and Margaret Denman and Jesus. The church was relatively empty this time. But because Jesus was there, the occasion mounted far greater in our hearts than the first wedding, as magnificent as it was.

Beginning then, our lives changed drastically. Rather than the big liquor parties which we once had in our home, we had Bible studies. Family devotions became a normal part of our lives. Church attendance no longer existed as an option for us; we never missed. God began to give me the opportunity to share my testimony in various churches. Within a year after Foy and I were remarried, we were conducting a family life seminar upon invitation in local churches. I enjoyed and appreciated the privilege of preaching from time to time. Through it all, God drew our family closer together. My hunger for His Word increased.

In August of 1972, the Paige Cothrens sold the last remaining supermarket; closed up the home; moved to Memphis; rented an apartment; and enrolled at Mid-South Bible College to prepare for a ministry wherever God wanted to send us. Five years later I graduated from Seminary, and Foy graduated from Mid-South.

May I conclude my testimony by saying here what I said at the beginning? In spite of all the "I's," Foy and I are aware that there was no good thing in either of us. It was Jesus and His work on the Cross which made everything possible. It was His grace by which He offered salvation to us. We can only say with all others who have trusted Him, "Thank You, Lord."

At the writing of this testimony, my family is complete. Foy, Fran, Jay, and I are all saved. Fran is married to a fine young man, Chris Hubbard. God has blessed them with our first grandson, Christopher Bradford Hubbard. All is well with my soul! Thank You, Jesus.

I APPLICATION

1 Do you remember the time (not the exact date necessarily) when you gave yourself to Jesus?

2 Are you certain you have done that?

3 If you haven't, why don't you do it now? Just give yourself to Him, and covenant with Him to spend your life serving Him in obedience to the Scriptures.

4 Have you ever shared (told) your testimony with anyone else?

5 What is your attitude toward your testimony? Are you concerned that it might not be as unusual as Paige Cothren's? Should you be?

6 Which miracle is greatest: Paige Cothren becoming a Christian or you becoming one?

7 How grateful are you to Jesus for taking your punishment for sin upon Himself? Very grateful? Grateful? Appreciative? Indifferent?

8 Have you expressed your gratefulness to God lately? Why don't you do that now?

9 Has salvation made a difference in your lifestyle? What difference?

10 Do you possess a desire to study the Bible? Witness to others concerning your faith? Pray? Fellowship with other believers? Do you do these things each day?

11 What has happened to your relationship with your unconverted friends since you became a Christian? Has it changed? How?

12 List the old "desires" that have gone away and the new desires which have replaced them, since you gave yourself to Jesus. (2 Corinthians 5:17)

13 Since salvation, has there been a change in your attitude toward church? Family? Former "enemies?" Others?

14 Compare the power in your life now to before salvation (2 Timothy 1:7)

15 According to 2 Timothy 1:7, what three qualities should now be present in your life? Where do these things originate?

16 What difference has your becoming a Christian made in the world for which Christ died?

II

MAN'S MISSING INGREDIENT

A Dream

Throughout the early years of my life I looked forward with great hope to the possibility of playing professional football. For me as a boy growing up at Mama Poole's, isolated in the green forests of South Mississippi, playing pro football was the zenith of all human endeavor. My favorite professional team then was the New York Giants. As mentioned earlier, my uncle, Buster Poole, had played for the Giants. Two other uncles also played with New York. Ray, the second oldest son, had begun his pro career with New York then retired from Montreal in the Canadian Football League. Barney, the youngest, had started his career with the old New York Yankees of the All-American Conference; moved to Dallas with the team for its one year there (1952) as the Texans; and then on to Baltimore with the Colts. But he finished his career with the Giants. The memory of our family huddled around the old radio on Sunday afternoons, frantically listening for the voice of the Giant announcer via short wave, lingers with me still. The concern of our hearts during those days was not whether the Giants won or lost their games. We rejoiced at just being able to "pick up" the broadcasts.

A Dream Come True

Being drafted by the Rams, however, wasn't all that bad. In 1957 Hollywood was still very much alive. The movie capital was at that time probably the most glamorous city in which to play professional football. The Los Angeles Coliseum usually filled for the Ram games. Movie stars were everywhere. Red Skelton's "Freddy the Freeloader" shack was sometimes set up on our practice field and scenes for his television show would be shot there. Practice would, of course, be halted and the players allowed to watch the scenes being filmed. Famous movie stars like Randolph Scott and Scott Brady were often seen in the Rams' dressing room. Bob Hope was one of the owners of the club and was occasionally visible to the players. On top of all that, my holder (I was a place kicker) was Elroy "Crazy Legs" Hirsh. Crazy Legs, as he was affectionately called because of his most unusual way of running, was a famous man. Several years prior to my entrance into the National Football League, a full-length movie of his life was shown in theaters everywhere and I had seen it. Just to be on the same field with Crazy Legs Hirsh was a thrill almost beyond description for me.

So you see, it was with a great deal of bewilderment, amazement, and wonder that I discovered that professional football, even Hollywood-style professional football, brought neither joy, happiness, nor peace into my life. I couldn't understand it! Since childhood my dream had been to do precisely what I found myself doing in 1957, playing professional football.

A nagging emptiness, an incompleteness appeared in my heart. Something vital was missing. I had no idea what it was. But with the passing games, the evidence became conclusive. Professional football had not brought meaning and purpose into my life. To seek Christian counsel, or any counsel for that matter, never occured to me. To have done so would have been to admit that I needed help. No tough, self-respecting professional football player would have confessed to that! But I grew more miserable by the week. The only times I was happy at all was during the games (probably because I was within hearing of the roar of the crowds), or when someone recognized me and asked for my autograph. Outwardly, of course, my unhappiness wasn't visible. But inwardly, a seething restlessness gripped my soul. Although my attitude in Los Angeles could best be described as being a jumbled mass of emotions (feelings, as commonly called), several of those emotions were distinguishable. I experienced periods of deep depression and hopelessness and I developed a severe temper, especially with Foy. I know now that I had depended upon Foy, as I had relied on football, to make me happy. When neither did, I grew frustrated and angry; but since I would have appeared to be rather foolish lashing out against pro football, I took most of my frustrations out on Foy. When frustration and anger are joined to man's old nemesis and Satan's old weapon, pride, destruction is imminent (Proverbs 16:18). Oh, the pride I had in my heart. I had lifted myself up by my bootstraps. I had made good! I played professional football!

Pride—Man's Downfall

Years later, after I had retired from professional football, that same pride got me into a lot of trouble. One of the Ram players with whom I had become very close was Larry Morris. Likewise, Larry's wife, Kay, and Foy were close friends. After several years with Los Angeles, Larry had been traded from the Rams to Chicago and then to Atlanta. He telephoned me from Atlanta one day. He and Kay had become avid snow skiers and wanted Foy and me to go skiing with them, along with a group of their friends from Atlanta.

I had never been on skis, but because I was constantly looking for a new "kick," Foy and I decided to go. We drove to Atlanta and on to North Carolina with Larry and Kay. When we arrived at the resort I found, much to my dismay, that there was not a drop of whiskey on the mountain. Not only that, but I discovered with horror, on the very first night, that the ski trip was some kind of a religious retreat, complete with nightly gospel singing, something called testimonies, and preaching. Actually, the preaching was probably Bible study, but at that time Foy and I didn't know the difference. I couldn't believe it! I thought, "I didn't travel all the way to North Carolina to go to church. Everything has its place and this certainly isn't the place for this!" To be sure, I didn't say anything to Larry, I just thought it.

To add misery onto misery, there was no snow. The temperature, however, was to be well below the freezing mark that night and the resort keepers assured us that one slope would be covered with snow the following day, the result of a technological marvel. Snow would actually be created by mixing certain chemicals with water and spraying it on the slope. I had never heard of that. But much to our delight, early the next morning, the slope was covered. The ski lift was not the kind of lift I had seen the skiers on television ride. This one was a rope-pull lift. Simply put, it was a large rope which, when held, would actually ski you up the slope. Before long we realized the slope would be extremely crowded, it being the only slope with snow. So when Larry suggested that I might want to take a skiing lesson with all the others who had never skied, I quickly refused. "I'll teach myself," I said. I was anxious to get onto the slope before it got crowded. Foy and the others were almost adamant. They insisted that I take a lesson. I thought to myself, "Don't they remember that I played pro football?" "Foy," I said, "I'm not going to waste my time letting that puny little ol' foreigner in his tight pants tell me what to do." I herded Foy and the others on to take their lesson, made my way over to the lift, and got in line to catch it. By the time my turn came, I had had the opportunity to watch several people catch the lift.

One nice thing about catching a rope lift, I soon realized, was that you could turn loose of the rope any time you wanted. That is what I did. I turned it loose just at the point where the mountain arched up at a sharp angle, about a hundred yards from the bottom edge of the snow where the line formed to catch the lift. I caught the lift several times and half-skiied and half-pushed myself, ever so slowly, down the gentle part of the slope. I was standing in line to catch the lift for the fourth or fifth "daring" trip when I felt a hand around my shoulder. It was Larry.

"I have never seen anything like it," he said.

I thought I knew what he was talking about. He was talking about me! I "knew" that "every eye on the slope had been on me." I was aware that I was "doin' good."

He repeated, "I have never seen anything like it."

"What's that?" I asked, cleverly concealing my pleasure.

"You," Larry said.

"Me?" I asked, acting completely surprised.

"You," he repeated. "Paige," Larry proclaimed, "I have been coming over here five years and I have never seen anyone catch on as quickly as you have."

"Oh, come on, Larry," I replied, in my heart really agreeing with him. I knew I had really learned to ski quickly. After all, I played pro football.

"No, it's true. Paige, you are already skiing as well as I am. Some people are just natural skiers. You are just a natural skier."

"Well, I did put a lot of thought into it before I came over here," I confidently laughed.

"You're ready for the top."

"I don't know, Larry," I answered. I did know though. I agreed with Larry. I was good. I knew it, and I was ready to come down from the top. "How ridiculous to suggest that a natural skier take lessons," I thought.

"I don't know, Larry," I repeated, not wanting to openly flaunt my massive amount of self-confidence.

"Yep, you're ready," he said again. "You're wasting your time down here on the beginners' slope."

"I don't know!"

"Come on," he insisted, "we'll go up together."

We got to the top of the mountain, finally, and I turned and got my first view downward. The cabins at the base of the slope looked like match boxes. The skiers catching the lift didn't look like people at all. "Were it not for their brightly colored clothes," I thought, "you couldn't even tell they were people," even though the line stretched all the way across the slope.

There comes at least one time in every lost man's life, I suppose, when his common sense to some degree makes an inroad into his pride. The confident smile left my face, in spite of my effort to keep it there.

"I don't know about this, Larry," I blurted out.

"No problem," Larry said, "it looks a lot steeper from up here. You'll find out on your way down that it's not much steeper than the bottom part. You're just seeing the whole slope at once from up here."

"That makes sense. Here I go!"

And I went—fast, with skis parallel. I don't know how fast a five-foot ten-inch, 210-pound man can go down a mountain on a pair of skis, but whatever it is, that's how fast I went. One miracle about that trip down is that I didn't fall. Another one is that I didn't hit anybody. The news about the runaway skier must have preceded me. People yelled and other people got out of the way.

"Snowplow!" someone yelled at me as I went by.

"Snowplow? Did he say snowplow? What's a snowplow?" I thought.

The line of skiers at the lift was getting closer and closer. People were yelling, "Snowplow!"

When I got within about seventy-five yards of the skiers who were lined all the way across the slope, I decided it was time to stop. So mentally I started slowing down. But physically, nothing changed.

"How do I stop?" I thought. There was nothing else to do but "hit the dirt." But I didn't hit it in time. On my back, skis and ski poles in the air, I slid straight into the line of skiers.

What a mess! Skis and people lay all over the hillside. Suddenly a hand reached down and rudely pulled the ski poles from my wrists. The little Austrian ski instructor was furious. "You kil' someone wit thees poles," he yelled, "you cannot haf theem any more."

I was trying to help people get up and get their skiis back on when I heard it: deep laughter, so deep that the person laughing seemed to be gasping for breath. I looked up the slope, and there was Larry, lying on his back, slowly sliding down the mountain, laughing. Then I understood. From the first phone call inviting me to come, he had "set me up."

Pride, that cursed characteristic found in every man's old nature, had gotten me into trouble. Pride occupied a very visible place in my life.

Why Couldn't I Be Happy?!?!

The question persists, though, why were Foy, marriage, and professional football not enough to satisfy me? Those observing my life probably couldn't understand why I wasn't blissfully happy. As a matter of fact, I couldn't understand why I wasn't happy either, and this added to my frustration. I seemed to have everything: money, a young attractive wife who loved me, and a name and reputation, at least in the sports world. What was that missing ingredient?

> God said, Let us make man in our image, after our likeness: and let them have dominion over the fish of the sea, and over the fowl of the air, and over the cattle, and over all the earth, and over every creeping thing that creepeth upon the earth. (Genesis 1:26)

And again,

And God blessed them, and God said unto them, Be
fruitful, and multiply, and replenish the earth, and subdue
it: and have dominion over the fish of the sea, and over the
fowl of the air, and over every living thing that moveth
upon the earth. (Genesis 1:28)

God seemed to have built the characteristic,
tendency, or desire to "rule and subdue" into the
very nature of man. Even though Scripture declines
to elaborate upon the "how," we read that man was
to dominate fish, fowl, cattle, every creeping thing,
and every living thing. Mankind was called to be a
keeper of all that God had created. Somehow,
supernaturally, everything would obey man. When
man wanted fish for food, fish might swim to the
edge of the water, to be easily caught. When he
desired fowl, the fowl would be easily captured.
The supernatural power by which these "miracles"
would be accomplished supposedly would be provided by the Supernatural One Himself, God.
Mankind's lot, then, was to be an easy one, our
reward for complete allegiance to our Creator.

A Bent to Rule

Thus, as surely as you and I inherited from our
first parents, Adam and Eve, physical and non-
physical attributes, we inherited from them an urge
to control our little part of the world. That seems to
be the message of Genesis 1:26 and 1:28.

But wait! Is man in control? Obviously he
doesn't control the fish and the fowl. Many millions
of dollars are spent each year in America on fishing

and hunting equipment. Neither fish nor fowl will come to man, and in fact both flee from him. The same thing can be said about most other wildlife.

Is man therefore capable of ruling his part of the world? Does he have dominion over his surroundings? If you have lived in this world for any length of time it may be as clear to you as it is to me that man has control of very little around him. Scripture produces the same answer. The writer of Hebrews says,

> What is man, that thou art mindful of him? or the son of man, that thou visitest him? Thou madest him a little lower than the angels; thou crownedst him with glory and honour, and didst set him over the works of thy hands: Thou hast put all things in subjection under him, he left nothing that is not put under him. BUT *NOW* SEE NOT YET ALL THINGS PUT UNDER HIM. (Hebrews 2:6-8, emphasis mine)

God, as has been stated, has placed into the nature of man a characteristic, a desire, yes, even a need in a limited sense to control his surroundings. He, that is, God, would live with and in man; He would walk with him in the cool of the day; and He would supply the power necessary for man to perform his God-appointed tasks. But after a while man rebelled against God. Sin entered into the world. "Wherefore, as by one man sin entered into the world, and death by sin; and so death passed upon all men, for that all have sinned." (Romans 5:12) Adam and Eve opened the door for sin to enter into the world and into every descendant, save One. God departed from man.

The consequences of God's departure from man were significant. Death became a frightening part of man's experience. The sin nature became an inherent part of man. Self became supreme, rather than God. And man's source of power was gone. Man's power was gone! But man's desire to rule and subdue was not. What had been lost was his power with which to accomplish it.

Truly, man was in a strait! Built into his nature by God Himself was a deep desire to rule and to subdue, but now he had no power with which to do it. What conflict flooded the mind of man! What void entered into his soul. Man could no longer do that for which, in part at least, he had been created.

An important relationship exists in man as well as in animals, between nature (desire) and performance. We have at our home two grey dogs, Puli, or Pulik as they are called in the plural. They are Hungarian sheep dogs. A book has been written about these unusual dogs which describes certain of their characteristics and habits. They are, for example, noted for their unusual loyalty to their masters. To capture this characteristic, we named the female "Sherah," for "loyal." In addition they possess an unusual ability to actually run across the backs of sheep in order to turn them in a given direction. Especially intelligent dogs, some, according to the book, have been able to learn and respond to over seventy-five different commands. And, in addition, they are good watchdogs. They bark. As a matter of fact they bark quite often. They bark at cars pulling up in the driveway. They bark at closet doors closing. They bark when someone, even a family member, walks down the stairs. They bark when the doorbell rings. And they go wild when a stranger enters the home. Barking is a part of their nature, their "early warning system" to alert the sheepherder that danger approaches. Every little sound, to a Puli, furnishes notice to bark, and he is happiest, the book states, when he does that which his nature craves to do. But we have neighbors.

I have tried to stop my dogs from barking. I have fussed at them. I have spanked them. I have even held their jaws together. While I can reduce the intensity of the sound, even holding their jaws together doesn't stop them from barking. They just emit a muffled bark. Eventually they become frustrated, as I attempt to suppress their natural tendency to bark. (Sometimes, I become frustrated when they don't stop barking.)

Allow me hurriedly to say that I am not comparing dog with man in order to learn truths about man. I'm illustrating simply how nature in living beings has a tendency to control, whether it be the nature of a Puli controlling her or the nature of man controlling him. Just as it is a Puli's nature to bark, so it is man's nature to rule and to subdue.

Unregenerate man discovers that he has no control over the fish, fowl, or the earth. He finds that he has little control over his occupational situation, his employees. Employees work with little control over their environment. Even the unions, seeking to give some control to the employees, have drained away control in other areas. Employers find themselves at the mercy of employees and the unions. All three must submit to the control of governmental authority. Man discovers that he has limited authority in the home. The husband and wife are often in conflict with one another. Often both are in conflict with the children, who might tend to be (and often are) rebellious toward their parents. Finally man realizes that he has little control over his own emotions. He has problems with his temper and various lusts. He lashes out at others with his tongue. Occasionally the conflict even becomes physical. Frustration ensues and he slides into despair and depression. Hope vanishes. Life has little meaning for him. He often fails to discover a purpose for his life.

Frustration

Because man is frustrated at being incapable of doing that which his very nature compels him to do, and with the absence of purpose and hope, deep dissatisfaction (or emptiness) settles into him. Frustration and dissatisfaction lead man on a search, a search for something or someone that will satisfy. Some men seem to gain a measure of satisfaction from sports. Many turn to immoral sex. Others depend upon money. Still others gain limited, albeit temporary, satisfaction through the escapism of music. Some gamble. Drugs and alcohol are tested to determine if perhaps they might satisfy the void, the emptiness, the incompleteness. Many turn to marriage, to a mate. Surely that one will provide motivation for life, they surmise.

When all of these things fail to provide on a permanent basis that which is missing, the search widens; other things are tested. As each new thing is tried, excites, and then fades away into failure, frustration increases, hope declines. Probably no one in the world is so miserable as the person who has sampled all the world's suggestions for happiness and who has watched each one systematically fail. When all the things have been tried and have failed, what then?

However, someone might ask, "Does any man ever actually have the oportunity to test all of the things which the world offers?" The answer is probably, "Not many, if any." A man's search will usually be limited by three situations or conditions: his time, his money, and cultural/social acceptance. A wealthy, self-employed man will, therefore, most likely be capable of searching into more "areas" than a moderately-salaried man, who, as the salary indicates, works for other people. The obvious reason is that the wealthy self-employed man has both more time and usually more money with which to search. The third element, though, does not restrict according to financial position. It affects everyone who lives within a given culture. If the culture approves adultery as an acceptable lifestyle, then adultery might become part of man's search. Several years ago in the South, a merchant who was caught in adultery might well lose his business. Today, even in small Southern towns, adultery doesn't make much difference any more; thus men likely attempt to satisfy their emptineess through sexual immorality.

Interestingly, wealthy people also commit suicide, their final act of frustration. The more things which fail, the more dissatisfied and hopeless man becomes. Depression and hopelessness, therefore, come not because of opportunities missed, but by the failure of "the tried" to give satisfaction and purpose to life.

What, Then, Does Satisfy?

Life's missing ingredient, therefore, may not be found in this world nor in its goods. It comes from doing, in part at least, that for which I was created, or ruling and subduing my little part of the world. However, a man (and I speak generically, for what is true for a male is true for a female as well) can only experience God's purpose for him when his unregenerate spirit has been brought back to life by the Holy Spirit of God, as he exercises saving faith in God's provision for sin, Jesus Christ. Then and only then can man gain a degree of control. Upon the institution of rule and control over the various elements of a man's life, his purpose for existence has been met. The restlessness which initially drove him into the search will begin to fade away before the influx of peace, contentment, and personal satisfaction which comes from doing that for which he was created. The search ends because the missing ingredient has been found.

I really believe that my restlessness, a result of not doing that for which I was created, propelled me through marriage and professional football, yet without finding satisfaction and purpose for my life. Existing within me could be found an incompleteness, a dissatisfaction, a longing, an emptiness. I was miserable because I was incomplete, even in the midst of all that this world offered.

The exciting news is that when I fell upon my knees, rule and control, therefore purpose and hope, became available to me. The reason, of course, was because God's power was given to me, through the ministry of the Holy Spirit (2 Timothy 1:7). Now, once again, I had power to accomplish God's purpose for me. First, I began to have control over my emotions. No longer was I compelled to "fly off the handle." The very same situations which had thrown me into angry tirades before, no longer did. I could laugh at myself now, something I had never been able to do.

The next affected area was my family. While my children were hurt terribly because of what I had done to them, there was at least respect, if not a deep love, for me. However reluctantly, they began to obey me. Foy, of course, had new respect for me. She, like I, began experiencing the same kind of phenomena, although perhaps to a lesser degree. Her sin and restlessness had not been as great as mine.

My employees also began to respond to me differently. Whether it was because the restlessness in my soul had been calmed or due to the fact that I responded differently to them, I don't know. I suppose both might be true. Whatever the reason, working conditions at my store were much more pleasant. I'm certain each of my former employees would agree.

Finally, the people of the community in which I lived began to respond to me. I found that whereas before, my opinion mattered little, now people would at least consider my views on various things.

Can you see what happened? As a Christian I began to experience, not a lordship control, but an authority stemming from my new-found respectability. As a Christian, I had regained a lot of control which had been lost by Adam in the fall of man.

This discussion closes with mention that the void in man's soul can only be filled when he is doing that for which he has been created. The power and authority by which he can accomplish it must come from God through the ministry of the Holy Spirit, after Jesus Christ is invited to come into his life. Man will never in this life be restored to his pre-fall state in relation to total rule and authority. (Note: However, in the Millennium, man will regain total control, for then"... the lion shall eat straw like the bullock," Isaiah 65:25.) He can, though, in Jesus, gain control to satisfy the yearning which God, at the time of creation, placed within him. Yet when man fails to receive the Lord Jesus Christ, the emptiness remains. Therefore the search continues. Marriage may become part of the search. Consequently man and woman often enter into the marriage relationship, each actually "using" the

other as the object of the search. This exerts a
tremendous amount of pressure upon each of them.
After all, the man, as does the wife, supposes that his
new partner is the "find" which will fill the emptiness. When both discover that the other one has
not fulfilled all that was expected of him or her,
serious problems begin to appear within the relationship. The problems which the wife often faces
will be discussed in Chapter Three. The husband's
problems will be examined in Chapter Four.

II APPLICATION

1 What have you learned from reading this chapter that you did not already know? Has reading it made a difference in your life?

2 Have you ever noticed an incompleteness in your life? Could the incompleteness be characterized as restlessness?

3 With what did you try to fill your life in order to satisfy the restlessness? List the things on a sheet of paper.

4 Did these "things" furnish any permanent joy or peace? Why not?

5 Read Genesis 1:26, 28 again, replacing the noun "man" and the pronoun "them" with your name? Can you find joy and peace and satisfaction there?

6 What degree of control do you have over your temper? Sensual desires? Tongue? Should you, as a Christian, be able to control these things?

7 How are you viewed by your family? Do you enjoy a real influence in the other members' lives?

8 Do your peers respect your opinion? Do they often ask for your advice?

9 How can you possess the partial control (over emotions, family, peers, etc.) which God has made possible for you to enjoy?

10 How can you realize that God wants you to accomplish that for which He created you? Will you determine to respond to people in love, thus setting the stage for mutual respect.

11 Has the search (for that which satisfies) ended for you? In Jesus, it can.

III

THY DESIRE SHALL BE TO THY HUSBAND!

A Thread of Similarity

In practically all of my counseling sessions involving marital breakdown there is a thread of similarity which runs through them. The trend surfaced in Foy's life and in mine, as well as both men and women counselees. Both will be fully discussed: The problem trend found in the woman will be examined in this chapter; the problem with the man in chapter four.

Before beginning the discussion though, permit me to say that these two trends, while they seem to have Biblical roots, may not be absolutes. They do, however, provide a "skeleton" of human behavior upon which the flesh of individual personality, situation, and activity may be exhibited quite differently. In other words, while this "skeleton" of male and female behavior remains essentially static, the manifestation of it may vary from person to person. Therefore I offer the "skeleton," not as static truth, but simply as a general guide which grants to us an insight into marital behavioral patterns of both men and women.

Genesis 3:16

Genesis 3:16 provides, it seems, a valuable glimpse into the personality of the woman, an insight which provides information leading us to an understanding of a new bride's attitude and behavior toward her husband. It reads:

> "Unto the woman He said, 'I will greatly multiply thy sorrow and thy conception; in sorrow thou shalt bring forth children; and thy desire shall be to thy husband, and he shall rule over thee.'"

You will recognize this verse of Scripture as the punishment which God levied upon the first woman Eve (and all her descendants) for her part in the original sin. The bulk of punishment was laid to the account of Adam, as verses 17-19 indicate, due probably to the fact that Adam sinned willingly, while Eve was deceived by a superior being. Adam, when confronted by his wife and enticed, deliberately and carefully chose to obey his wife rather than God. Certainly it was a hard decision for Adam. Perhaps it was one which you and I cannot comprehend. Had Adam chosen God, he might have wondered, whom would be his mate? There was no other woman. From my imagination, I can almost visualize Adam as he wrestled with his conflict. He must have looked at Eve and then at God; then Eve; then God. Finally he made his choice, unfortunately a wrong one splattered with eternal consequences.

The Punishment

"Unto the woman, He said, 'I will greatly multiply thy sorrow and thy conception . . . .'" The phrase might also read, "thy sorrow and thy pregnancy." In other words, God seems to be saying that the woman's lot was to be one of sorrow in that part of her life affected by conceiving children, or the marital state. Later in the same verse God says, "in sorrow thou shalt bring forth children." Here He emphasizes, apparently, the distinction between the former sorrow of the married state and the later sorrow of the physical pain of childbirth. The former sorrow seems to refer to the woman's lot in her marriage, that state which produces conception; the later sorrow almost certainly concerns the physical pain involved in giving birth to children.

If the above interpretation of the first two parts of woman's four-fold punishment is correct, then without a doubt here stands one of the great verses of prophetic truth in all the Bible. Indeed, historically in almost every culture since creation six thousand years ago, the woman's marital lot has been one of suffering. As a matter of fact, from creation to the giving of the law to Moses on Sinai, women generally were viewed as little more than the property of their husbands. In some lands he even had the right of life and death, not only over his wife (or wives as the case may be) but also over his daughters. When God gave the law to Moses, then in one culture at least, man was prohibited from killing his wife except when she was guilty of adultery (Leviticus 20:10 and Deuteronomy 22:22) or if she had professed to be a virgin and was later found not to be one (Deuteronomy 22:13-21). In the event a married woman committed adultery, Jewish law commanded the guilty man to be killed, also. However, Mosaic law remained unheeded in most cultures, and women were forced into total subjection to men.

When Jesus came, died, rose and went back to Heaven, He left many teachings about marriage relationships, many of which were founded upon the Mosaic Law. He also left the apostle Paul. It was through Paul that Jesus elevated woman higher than she had ever been. Paul's writings reflected woman's total equality with man in relation to her person, that is, "who she is." In relation to her role or responsibility within the marriage relationship there exists a chain of command, but in relation to her worthiness before God, the woman was lifted to total equality with man (1 Corinthians 7:4). (This concept will be discussed in depth in Chapter Five). Thus, wherever true Christianity has flourished, woman has been lifted to a status of equality with her husband. In many parts of the world Christ's teaching, however, remains unknown. There, a woman often continues to be nothing more than a piece of property.

Those teachers who proclaim that Paul hated women prove only their total lack of understanding and knowledge of the workings of Christianity as taught by Paul. When cultures are carefully examined women have been elevated by the love of God as expressed through Bible-centered Godly men, like Paul, not through civil law. Therefore, as mentioned earlier, Genesis 3:16 provides one of the Bible's most important prophetic truths. Certainly, the woman's lot since creation has been one of sorrow and suffering in her relationship with her husband.

The second act of punishment indicates that child-bearing, that is, the actual birth of the child, would involve pain. Apparently in the beginning it was not meant to be so. The original plan of God must have provided for childbirth to be at least painless, if not pleasant. Because sin came into the world through the woman however, and since the child comes into the world through the woman, the introduction of pain into the birth process might have been to remind us of the original sin and its entrance through mankind into the world.

At the birth of my first grandchild (and at this writing my only grandchild, although I am joyfully anticipating many others) I watched my daughter, Fran, endure labor pains for some twelve hours before delivering a beautiful, healthy son, Brad. I held her hand for several hours, willfully allowing her to squeeze mine, as the pains periodically increased in intensity and frequency. In one of the lulls between pains, I asked, "Honey, do you know why you are feeling this pain?" She quietly nodded her head, indicating "yes." I went on to explain that the pains were a result of sin, not hers necessarily, but Eve's. Fran's pains were a reminder, not only to Fran but to all of us who love her, that sin found its way into the world through her first mother, Eve.

The fourth part of the judgment upon the woman as recorded in Genesis 3:16 reads, "and he shall rule over thee." History once again has verified the accuracy of Scripture, for in many cultures the man has certainly controlled the woman. Little will be said about this point now because the meaning of the phrase will be examined completely in Chapter Five.

However, because female submission is mentioned in Genesis 3:16, two principles should be quickly addressed. First, when the Word of God teaches that the woman must be subject to the man, it means that she should submit to him in relation to what she does in the family unit as opposed to who she is. Secondly, the woman ought never submit her mind, emotions, or will to anyone nor anything save Jesus Christ. Again, these principles will be fully discussed in Chapter Five, a chapter entitled, "Upon Whom Should You Build Your Life?"

The Insight

The third part of the Genesis 3:16 passage is the one toward which we are heading. Here, God "opens a window" and allows all of us, even the woman, a glimpse into the very nature of the female. The phrase reads, "and thy desire shall be to thy husband . . . ." What does that mean to you? The verse seems to be teaching that as part of a woman's punishment for the original sin, she will desire her husband. But what does that mean? In what way will she desire him? Further, how does it give us an insight into her nature and how does it apply to woman today? Apparently the phrase means that every "normal" woman (that is, every woman not caught up in the sin of homosexuality) has built into her very nature a desire to respond to her husband. To say it another way, she possesses a great desire to give herself over to her husband in every way. In other words, every normal woman finds built into her very nature a desire to please her husband, or at least to please one man at a time. Obviously it is part of her punishment. But how is it part of her punishment? Included in her desire to please her husband, she discovers that she has a tendency to build her entire life around him. That means that she finds herself to be emotionally dependent upon her husband. Her emotional state, therefore, depends upon her relationship with him. Women with whom I have counseled have almost unanimously expressed a desire to yield themselves to their husbands emotionally, mentally, sexually and in all other ways. Most women, it seems, have in the beginning of the marriage relationship little desire to look at or to consider an intimate relationship with any other man. The new bride has but one primary ambition, that being to please her new husband.

Now, as I mentioned before, this characteristic is not a blessing for the woman. It is a curse. It tends to control a woman's entire emotional makeup, by thrusting her emotional state under her husband's control (although he may not be very conscious of it). Therefore, included in the desire to give herself totally to her husband comes a supersensitivity concerning everything he does, especially in relation to other women. With almost supernatural awareness, she becomes capable of picking up even the slightest vibration that something is amiss in the marriage relationship.

That capability was certainly evident in Foy's life. Before we became Christians, I enjoyed going to the wrong kind of parties. Foy reluctantly went with me. Some of these parties occurred at friends' homes, some at ours. One thing, though, was always certain. Following the party, Foy could recount from memory things completely beyond my ability to recollect. She could recite all that I had done at the party. She could name all the women with whom I had talked; she could list the order in which I had talked to them. She could recall how long I had talked to each of them. She even knew whether or not I initiated the conversation and if I enjoyed it. How could she do all of that? (Sometimes we men make jokes about our wives' "hawk eyes.") Wives seem to be capable of knowing everything we do. A wife might walk down the street with her husband and seem to be totally absorbed in window shopping. Her husband, thinking his wife isn't noticing him, might look at a woman across the street. Often, his wife will know it instantly. What the husband probably does not know is that his wife was conscious of the approaching woman even before he saw her. When the wife looked into the store window, she allowed her husband what seemed to be an opportunity to look at another woman. Her gaze into the store window in no way meant that she was oblivious to the other woman's presence. As a matter of fact, often a wife will appear to be oblivious to the presence of other women in order to discover whether or not, or the manner in which, her husband will look. We men might refer to that kind of behavior as "being set up," and rightly so, for that is precisely what happens. It is part of a wife's protective system, used to alert her concerning her husband's attitudes. But it also "burdens" her, often controlling her emotional state, thus proving to be a "curse."

The wife need not be overly condemned for the above conduct, although in Christ she need not be enslaved to it either. Her nature, as mentioned, entices her to act that way. Her emotions are distinctly tied to her husband. Her actions are simply natural responses to impulses and they are designed to remind the wife that this characteristic remains as part of her judgment for the original sin. It becomes an enslavement not particularly enjoyed by the woman. Certainly the husband almost always dislikes it. Many men upon being confronted by their wives with being "too interested" in other women charge their wives with being overly suspicious . "You don't trust me," they accusingly reply. For husbands to understand that this trait is inherent within the nature of their wives becomes extremely important. Hopefully a Christian wife will also recognize that she does not need to live a burdened life enslaved and possessed by a jealous nature. Jesus, the Last Adam, came into the world to reverse all that the first Adam had effected. Christ's life, death, burial, resurrection, and ascension back into Heaven as our Intercessor and Advocate have laid the groundworks whereby we might be free from the effects of the first Adam's sins, including that one. (There is, of course, one exception. All men, save that blessed generation who are alive at Christ's coming, must go through the doorway of physical death.)

At the beginning of this chapter I mentioned that there were two basic problems often manifested in marriage breakdowns, one in the woman, one in the man. These problems frequently occur simultaneously, although the man's problem often ignites the one in his wife. Both will be discussed at the end of chapter four, as they unfold in an actual marriage relationship. I will attempt there to illustrate the simultaneous effect of each one upon the other. However, in this chapter, which (as stated) deals with the wife's problem, i.e., her sensitivity toward her husband, I will begin the step-by-step process (hopefully) of explaining how that sensitivity influences her marriage.

The Application

When a young lady "takes a husband" she usually has, of course, very high and exciting expectations. The glamor of being a wife; the satisfaction of being able to give herself totally to a man who loves her and who treats her with great dignity, courtesy, and respect; the security of having a home and furniture; the excitement of learning to cook and serve meals; the romance of the nights alone with her husband; the expectations of being a mother, and many other anticipations all combine to create within her a great exuberance about being married. Within the limits of human possibility, she usually commits herself totally to her husband and to the marriage. Her commitment to her husband, however, does not in and of itself purify all her responses to him. There may be some selfishness and pride in her actions. For example, she might encourage her husband to hold her hand as they walk through the shopping center. Part of her reason might be to "announce" to all other women, "Hands off, this one is mine." Or she might wait for her husband to open the car door or expect him to seat her in a restaurant. Part of her subconscious motive might be that she wants others to notice the high favor in which she stands with her husband. So you see, all of the young bride's motives may not be perfect. Basically, though, she is commited to her husband and to the marriage.

The wife's commitment to the marriage, in contrast to that of most husbands, includes all of her: her emotions, her mind, her body are all committed to making the marriage work. I say that this is in contrast to the husband because in the beginning of the marriage usually he has not committed as much of his emotions or mind to the marriage as has his wife. Often, though, he commits more of his body to the sexual relationship than does his wife. However in other areas of physical commitment such as working around the house, time spent with his wife, etc., he expends perhaps a smaller amount of time. This may occur partly, at least, because the husband usually works outside the home.

As the marriage relationship begins, the wife's trait of sensitivity begins to be evident. She usually applies herself wholeheartedly to pleasing her husband and to making a good home for both of them. But after a few months, the new wife might begin to notice a change in her husband, a change of which he may be relatively unconscious. He doesn't seem to be as attentive to her as he was in the early days of the marriage. In those first days he would come in after work, throw his arms around her and demand (jokingly and enthusiastically) to know everything she had done that day. He was anxious to get her out of the house; to take her to a restaurant so she wouldn't have to cook dinner; to show her off. He would talk to her and answer her questions in a loving tone of voice. There was no doubt in her mind then of his affection for her, for he openly displayed it. Now, however, she begins to notice a change in him, a slight change to be sure, but a change. At first she may not be overly alarmed. She has probably heard about "the wearing off" syndrome, how the "new" will always wear off the marriage. Everyone experiences it, she reasons. There isn't really anything to worry about. But the trend continues. As the months pass and the newness of the marriage fades, her husband moves even farther away, often becoming less and less attentive. (Note: The reason for this movement is found in man's problem and will be discussed extensively in chapter four.) At some point in his movement away, the husband may not only stop responding to his wife positively but he may even begin to respond negatively. He might now come in from work and rather than placing his arms around his wife and asking her about her day's activities, plunge onto the couch and yell, "When's supper going to be ready?" The husband might begin to complain about having to work around the house. "After all," he declares, "I have been working hard all day." Those fewer and fewer times that he takes his wife out to dinner, he seems embarrassed at holding her hand. He almost never opens the car door for her any more and begins to be self-conscious when, because he and his wife approached the car on the rider's side, he knows he is expected to open it. Tender moments between them grow farther and farther apart, eventually almost completely disappearing. The sexual relationship becomes just a physical one for the wife, but because it is almost the only time any closeness occurs (if what is usually happening by now could be construed as closeness), she willingly participates in it (as time passes the wife may view these weekly visits into the bedroom as her being "used" and she may grow to resent it). About this time the wife's "antennae" of supersensitivity begin to rise. She wonders, "What is happening? Why doesn't he respond to me like he did before? Is there someone

else? What am I doing wrong?, etc., etc., etc. . . ."
Soon, the wife begins to verbalize her thoughts. She
questions her husband. She might even begin to
"nag" him slightly, hoping to get him to talk about
the situation, why they are drifting apart. When she
embarks upon this endeavor, that is, "nagging" (the
man usually refers to this action with other termin-
ology), the distance between them more often than
not widens; the tension increases; the antennae rise
higher and his attention toward her decreases. The
marriage is in trouble.

At this point a wife often experiences a physical
phenomenon. She might lose her desire to remain
attractive and "lets herself go" physically. Depression sometimes does this to a person; it causes her
not to care. The fact that her relationship with her
husband is not "right" even becomes evident upon
her face. She may conclude something like, "If he
doesn't care any more, then I won't either." (Note:
Sometimes a hurt wife will "punish" her husband by
depriving him of an attractive mate by "letting
herself go.")

In the beginning of this chapter, I mentioned
that a woman's emotions are often totally involved
with the man with whom she is sharing the intimacy
of her life. Sharing her life intimately with a man
involves, for the wife, much more than just doing
things together. For her, marriage is a state of being.
It usually includes becoming emotionally committed to the man. But once these emotions are hurt,
abused, and rejected and the woman believes that
there is no hope, she will probably grow extremely

bitter toward her husband, often toward life, and sometimes even toward herself and God. She may also turn those antennae away from her husband in search of another man upon whom she can best bestow all of her affection. Remember, God caused her to desire one man at a time. When she is convinced that her husband will not be that man, she might begin the search for another one. She really believes that she cannot be happy unless she is giving herself completely to a husband, to a marriage.

Both Foy and the great preponderance of women with whom I have had the privilege of counseling followed this same basic trail. As discussed previously the individual circumstances may vary from person to person but the general trend is almost always the same. Also, the time frames may differ from person to person. By that I mean that one woman may grow hopeless after six months of rejection; another woman after twelve months of rejection; another woman only after years of rejection. But usually there will come a time in every neglected wife's life when she thinks she must search elsewhere for someone upon whom to bestow all her affections.

The question may be appropriately asked, "Is what you say true for both Christian and non-Christian women alike?" It need not be. A Christian wife has all the resources and power of Heaven to enable her to endure far more pressure and rejection than an unsaved woman. After all, the Christian wife should build her life upon her Namesake, Jesus

Christ, not upon temporal things, including her husband. Therefore, she need not necessarily be compelled to live a life dependent upon the response of anyone, neither her husband nor any temporal thing. She can live above all her circumstances and possess joy and peace despite her husband's rejection. Again, Jesus can actually reverse that which Adam's sin caused God to implant within woman's nature. The situation is rather dim for an unsaved woman, though. She will almost certainly wrestle with that part of her nature all the days of her life and may find herself completely hopeless in her failure to control it.

After Foy had received the Lord Jesus Christ as Savior, that part of her nature was practically invisible, if indeed it was present at all. What a glorious day for both of us! To know that there would be no more suspicions, those ungodly thoughts which had been such a central part of our "pre-salvation" lives. Her trust in me went far beyond faith in a man. Because I had become a Christian, she began to trust God to keep me from sin. In addition to trusting God, her so-called "need" for my love, respect, and response to her became what it really was, a "want." She did not "need" Paige Cothren any more. She wanted me, but she did not "need" me. What a difference! Foy learned that whether I was in her life or out of it, her life would continue, because she was no longer building her life upon the "shifting sand" of a fickle human being, but upon the eternal Rock, the Lord Jesus. (This concept will be further discussed in chaper five.)

Foy's dependence upon the Lord, however, in no way diminishes my responsibility to her as her husband, nor hers to me as a wife. God still expected me, as He states in His Word, to obey Him in my role as a husband. The difference now was that Foy's emotional state did not depend upon my obedience. For her, "thy desire shall be to thy husband" became "thy faith hath made thee whole."

III APPLICATION

1 Mothers, have you ever thought about the purpose for pain in childbirth? When your children were born, did your family remember this purpose?

2 Wives, why not prove (test) Genesis 3:16? Be conscious of your own sensitivity toward your husband. In what areas of your life would you say you are more sensitive than he is? What problems does this sensitivity cause?

3 Wives, is your supersensitivity toward your husband a "product" of the old nature or the new nature? Was it evident before salvation? After salvation only? Both?

4 Wives, do you enjoy your husband's attentions and affections in the presence of other women? Why?

5 Wives, what erases your desire for intimacy with your husband fastest? An argument with him? Something else? Is your husband affected the same way? Why or why not?

6 Wives, do you *need, want, expect,* or *demand* attention from your husband at times other than times of intimacy? What is the difference between need and want? Would you say affluent America has confused the two? Have you?

7 Husbands, have you ever noticed in your wife a different kind of behavior, attitude, or reaction from that of yourself and other men? What is the difference? Why does she behave, think, and react differently from men? Have you adjusted your life to it? Do you ridicule her for it?

8 Wives, what would make you saddest? Losing your husband or your salvation? As a Christian, you need not be emotionally controlled by anyone except Jesus Christ. Who controls your emotions? Why not pray and commit your life to rest upon the foundation, Jesus Christ.

Wives, invite several ladies over for coffee and discuss the concepts included in this chapter with them. Ask them their views concerning their sensitivities toward their husbands.

IV

HONEY, I LUST AFTER YOU. LET'S GET MARRIED!

90% Man

Most likely this chapter will influence few husbands to claim me as a friend. Hopefully though it will cause them to examine the real reasons which prompted them to marry their wives. For I believe that the great preponderance of problems found in the beginning of a marriage breakdown can be laid to the account of the husband and his erroneous purpose for entering the marriage relationship. After making that statement, I know you wives are going to continue reading. Please husbands, you continue to read, too. I believe you will discover that what is written in this chapter may revolutionize the entire relationship between you and your wife.

You may reply, "That's a pretty rash statement to make, that most of the initial problems lie with the husband! Can you prove it?" I believe I can, but before I attempt to do so, there are certain foundations of truth which must be laid.

Satan Alters Words

First, Satan is the master of deceit and the father of lies. One of his primary strategies is to alter the meaning of words. "Alter the meaning of words?!" you say. Yes, Satan has learned to alter the meaning of God's key Biblical words through the passage of time, so that when we read them in the Bible, especially the authorized version (King James), we think something other than what our Lord would have us think. For example, when the Bible says, "Believe on the Lord Jesus Christ and thou shalt be saved" (Acts 16:31), what do you suppose the average unsaved person, and perhaps the average church member, supposes that the Bible means? What do you think? Today, in our culture, belief is a function of the intellect alone, an intellectual acknowledgment of something as truth. That is not, however, the original intent of the word. In the original language, the word "believe" is the verb form of the noun which translates "faith." The basic meaning, therefore, of the word "believe,' in regard to personal salvation, is "exercising faith" in Jesus, that is, casting your whole being into His hands. Now, that happens to be a much greater commitment than simply acknowledging with your mind that Jesus Christ is a real Person. It is a great deal more than believing with your intellect that He is God or even that He came into the world to pay the supreme penalty for your sins and for mine. Believing on the Lord Jesus Christ demands that you yield your life to Him through the exercise of your will, not only because you understand intellectually who He is and what He came into the world to do, but also because your heart was affected by it. Thus, "believe" involves three functions of a person's immaterial being: his intellect, his emotions, and his will. The average American probably "believes" in Jesus according to the cultural definition of the word believe. But the average American almost certainly isn't broken-hearted over Jesus' death nor has he, by an act of his will, yielded his life to our risen Lord. Do you wonder with me how many of our church members have "believed" on the Lord Jesus only with their intellects and mistakenly think, "All is well with my soul?" In conclusion, the twentieth-century English word "believe" just simply does not bring to mind all the meanings of the word, a word which our Lord used in telling us how to be rightly related to Him. Because this is so, it is the responsibility of every preacher and teacher of the Word of God to teach, in love, the difference between the two concepts of the word "believe." We ought to be very careful to explain to our listeners God's meaning of "believe." Our tasks have not been properly executed until we do. The destiny of souls might well depend upon it.

Please don't misunderstand me, as some people have done. I am not saying the King James translation is always wrong. The point I am attempting to make is this: The King James Bible was completed in 1611, as the introductory pages of your King James translation testify. Many words were used which either are not in our current American vocabulary or which actually have changed meanings through the years.

For instance, one word, used quite often in the King James version, is the Old English word "wot." There are many other words, "concupiscence," for example, which we simply do not use today. What does concupiscence mean? These two words and many others are not usually utilized in today's culture. Neither the King James translators nor God are at fault. The fact is that in the three hundred-plus years since the authorized Bible was completed, many words have fallen into disuse and are no longer in the vocabularies of the people. Likewise, many new words have come into our vocabularies, and many words have actually altered definitions. Therefore, in order to understand God's message, we must understand the meaning of words as they were originally employed. "Wot," by the way, normally means "know." "Concupiscence" is similar in meaning to our word "sensuality," a key word, incidentally, in understanding the cause of many marital problems today.

Not only have certain key words in the King James Bible fallen out of our American vocabulary but, as stated, other key words have actually changed meaning through the years. When we attach our modern meanings to these precious Old English words, we often fail to receive God's message. One good example is found in 1 Thessalonians 4:15. In this section of Scripture, beginning with verse 4:13 and continuing on to 5:11, Paul encourages believers not to despair over their dead

Christian brothers and sisters. Because Jesus died and rose again, Paul exhorts, ". . . even so them also which sleep in Jesus will God bring with him." (4:14) Then in the next verse, Paul explains, "For this we say unto you by the word of the Lord, that we which are alive and remain unto the coming of the Lord shall not PREVENT (emphasis mine) them which are asleep." Is Paul saying that the generation which is alive at the coming back of our Lord will not prevent the dead in Christ from going to Jesus? Even if they could, why would they want to do that? Of course they would not want to do that. God wrote the whole section to show that the dead in Christ, those beloved Christian relatives whose bodies are now in the grave, will rise from the grave to be with the Lord forever. The word "prevent," as recorded in verse 15, in the language of our culture would read "precede." Paul teaches that the generation which is alive when Jesus comes back shall not precede those who are dead in going into His presence. In other words, ". . . the dead in Christ shall rise first: then we which are alive and remain shall be caught up together with them in the clouds, to meet the Lord in the air: and so shall we ever be with the Lord." (4:16b, 15) That the word "prevent" actually means "precede" is verified in Psalms 88:14. There the Psalmist writes, ". . . and in the morning shall my prayer prevent (precede, or go before) thee" (parenthesis mine). Obviously man cannot prevent God from doing anything.

Another word, used in Paul's second epistle to the Thessalonians, has a completely reversed meaning since it was recorded in the King James Bible in 1611. Paul, explaining the end times, wrote that there shall come a day when apostasy will run rampant across the earth prior to the coming in judgment of the Lord Jesus. But this time of great evil, which will be initiated by the man of sin, the son of perdition (2 Thessalonians 2:7), shall not come until "... he who now LETTETH will LET, until he be taken out of the way" (emphasis mine). God, through Paul, reveals to us the truth that someone who is "LETTING" must be taken out of the way before the man of sin becomes completely manifested. But what does that mean? What does "letteth" mean? Who must be taken out of the way? If we apply the twentieth-century meaning to the 1611 word "letteth" we might never be able to untangle the mystery of the meaning of the verse. When, however, we discover that in 1611 the word 'letteth" or "let" meant "restrain," the secret becomes discernible. Again, please don't accuse me of saying that the King James Bible is wrong here. That isn't what I am saying. I am saying that since 1611, the common meaning of the word "let" has completely reversed. In 1611 it meant "restrain." Today it connotes "allow," meanings exactly opposite. To understand God's message to us, we must apply, not the modern American definition of the word "let" to that passage, for that reverses the meaning; rather, we must apply the 1611 meaning to it. God's intent then becomes clear. Who restrains sin in the world today? The Holy Spirit! When He is taken out of the way, in what scholars commonly call the "rapture" of the saints (or perhaps more properly, the translation of the saints), sin will be free to run rampant across the face of the earth. The Holy Spirit Who lives in believers will deliver us all into the very presence of the Lord. When the Holy Spirit departs, then all righteousness will be gone from this planet, and Satan will be free to perpetrate evil at will. The key to understanding this verse, however, depends upon understanding the meaning of the Old English word "let."

Finally, we should examine one word, found in 1 Peter 3:1-2, before we see how this all applies to the husband. The word is "conversation." To you and me the word conversation means to communicate to another person or persons by means of spoken words, or talk. Verse one, though, indicates perhaps a different meaning or at least an additional meaning. What our Lord seems to be saying through the apostle Peter essentially is this: If any women have unsaved husbands they may without a word win their husbands by their conversation. Now, obviously if you and I accept the modern definition of the word conversation we have a problem. How can a wife win her husband to the Lord through her conversation without speaking a word? Apparently the word conversation meant something more than talking. To the audience in 1611, the word conversation probably meant to converse with others through every means, including actual talk, but primarily through conduct. Therefore, the passage, for us today, would probably better read ". . . that, if any obey not the word, they also may without a word be won by the conduct (including conversation, of course) of the wives; while they behold your chaste conduct coupled with fear" (1 Peter 3:1b-2, parenthesis mine). An additional "argument" for this interpretation is found in the word "behold." Talk cannot be beheld; conduct can be.

These words are but a few of a rather large number to be found in the King James version of the Bible which either are not in our present vocabularies or which have actually changed meaning through the years. You might ask, "If that is true, how can a layman who has never studied Hebrew or Greek study the King James Bible with confidence?" Might I answer with two suggestions? If there is a question in your mind about the meaning of a word in your authorized Bible, mark it and ask your preacher or Bible teacher about it. Or you may want to do as I do and refer to a good, modern translation. I am not advocating that you should discard the King James Bible. What I am suggesting is that you might want to refer to a good modern translation, like the New American Standard, in conjunction with your King James Version. Each morning in my devotion and Bible study I open my New American Standard Bible to the same passage that I am studying in my King James edition. When I read a passage or a word that I don't understand, I refer to the New American Standard. If that doesn't satisfy me then I might do further research into the original language. In no case should we proceed in our study until we fully understand what God is saying. The Word of God was given for our obedience. We cannot obey it until we understand it. Consequently we must know the meaning of words.

Back To The Problem

Now, let us go back to the husband and what I believe is the great problem in the early days of most marriages today. Ephesians 5:25 tells husbands to ". . . love your wives even as Christ also loved the church, and gave himself for it." Apparently the key word in that passage is "love." Carefully now, what is the meaning of love?

For what it is worth, I am convinced that the world does not know the meaning of the word. I am just as convinced that many Christians do not really understand the meaning of the word love. Of the hundreds of people with whom God has given me the privilege of counseling, only a handful have defined the word love. That is phenomenal in view of the fact that "it was love that took my place on the cross of Calvary," as the old hymn declares. Love is "the mark of a Christian" according to Francis Schaeffer, a contemporary author who has so entitled one of his books. "It was love that drew salvation's plan . . . it was grace that brought it down to man," another popular hymn reminds us. Love is God's word and His concept. He coined the word and made it one of the key words in the Christian faith. "For God so loved the world, that He gave His only begotten Son . . . ." (John 3:16) Love is the motivating force which prompted God to offer His son upon the altar of sacrifice in order to give an undeserving race of beings a way into His eternal presence. It is love for one another by which all men are to recognize that Christians are Jesus' disciples. (John 13:35) Love motivates us to obey our Lord. "... If a man love me, he will keep my words (commandments)," Jesus says (John 14:23, parenthesis mine).

Be it far from me to dogmatically declare that love is the most important word in the revelation of God to man, but no doubt it must be included as one of the most important. No wonder that the Evil One has declared war upon the word. If Satan succeeds in concealing God's definition of love and is able to insert his own definition into the minds of God's people, what a victory he will have won!

Several years ago now I turned on the television set late one night. I was looking for a good Western movie or perhaps a good documentary film. As I turned from channel to channel, I passed by a popular late night panel talk show. I never watch that particular program, which is shown each week night, but that night something one of the panelists said caught my attention as I flipped the channel selector past the channel on which the program is shown. Quickly turning back, I listened with a great deal of interest to the discussion. The panelists were attempting to define love. One of them said that "love is a feeling." Now that was an interesting statement. We "feel" with our sense of touch. How can you feel love? As a matter of fact, the meaning of the word "feeling" has also been altered so that it has completely lost its original meaning. A man may say something like, "I feel like I ought to go to church tomorrow!" What has he said? Is he going to church tomorrow or not? I dare say I do not know. He really hasn't conveyed any meaning. "Feeling" is a non-committal word. It has infiltrated our vocabularies, allowing us to talk without saying anything. The use of it requires no commitment and produces no guilt. If the man had said what he really meant he probably would have said, "I *know* I ought to go to church tomorrow," or "I *think* I ought to go to church tomorrow." If he had said either of the two statements, he would have made a commitment, at least in what he knew he should do. Then, not to have gone to church when he knew he should have gone, and had so stated, would have produced guilt. Love, a feeling? No, love cannot be a feeling.

Another of the panelists probably got closer to the truth. He said, "Love is an emotion." What he seemed to be saying was that love is a function of man's emotions.

There are three basic parts to man's immaterial being. (His material being, of course, is his physical body.) His imaterial parts are those which are not physical. They include his intellect, his emotions, and his will. Man can say and understand the words, "I am, I ought, I will." He possesses self-consciousness (I am); self-determination (I ought); and self will (I will). An animal cannot do any of the three. Animals function on the basis of impulse. But man is different. He can think and plan and finally choose a course of action.

Is love then a function of man's emotion? No doubt, a person's emotions are involved when he loves. But is love a function of his emotions principally? No, real love extends far beyond a person's emotions.

A third panelist declared that love is a "happening." That definition of love is perhaps the most popular one and probably the one with which Satan is most pleased. It is likewise probably the most deceptive of all. A happening is something over which one has no control. It just happens. Concerning love we say, "I fell in love." When we so state our entrance into love we are actually saying that something happened to me over which I had no control. I "fell uncontrollably" into a relationship of love. May I suggest that if you fell into it you had better crawl out of it because it isn't love.

Picture in your mind for a moment if you will a married man working in an office with several women. He begins to have an adulterous relationship with one of them and decides he wants to marry her. Asking his wife for a divorce, he says, "I have fallen in love with someone else. I didn't mean to. It just happened!" What is the man actually saying? The excuse which he is offering to his wife is that something happened to him quite beyond his ability to either prevent or to control. An outside, overwhelming force overtook him and compelled him to do what he did. "Don't blame me," he is suggesting. "I couldn't help it. It's not my fault."

Much of the modern world accepts the above concept as a valid one. "After all," our society declares, "if you fall in love with someone other than your wife or husband, you have a right to live with that person." The fact that a divorce must occur is no reason, the world declares, to forsake the one you "love!"

Wait a minute! If love is a happening over which the one doing the loving has no control, how then can our loving God command us to love? Would the One Who loved us so much that He was willing to allow His Son to suffer His wrath against sin in our place, actually command us to do something beyond our abilities, and then judge us guilty for not doing it? Would God order me to lift my house with my bare hands, or command me to flap my arms and fly like a bird? I cannot do either of those things! For God to command me to do the impossible and then condemn me for not doing it would appear to be unjust and foreign to the nature of God! God is not unjust. Nor will He command me to do something beyond my power to do. Yet He commands me to love.

Love Is A Command

". . . Love thy neighbor as thyself," God commands (Matthew 19:19). He expects us to love our Christian brother and sister (John 15:12-17). "Husbands, love your wives, even as Christ also loved the church . . . ." (Ephesians 5:25) Love your enemies, He demands. (Luke 6:27-35) Finally He beseeches us to love Him with all our heart, soul, and mind (Matthew 22:37). God commands people to love.

He commands you to love. If love is a happening over which we have no control, how can He do that? Of course, the answer is simple. Since God commanded us to love, we can *will* to love. Therefore, love is a function primarily of our wills, not of our intellects, nor of our emotions. Certainly both of these immaterial characteristics are involved, especially after we choose to obey God. But love is basically a function of the human will.

God gave to Foy and me a firsthand illustration of just how our intellect and especially our emotions are affected in a marital relationship when, after we exercised our wills, He blessed us through our obedience to Him. Stuart Angle, the dear Christian who led us to Christ, taught us what the Bible had to say about divorce, remarriage, and the will of God. Through the study of God's Word we slowly began to understand that God wanted us to remarry. But, humanly speaking, we had little desire to live with one another again. There was no "physical" desire left in either of us. When we considered remarriage, there were no squealing sirens in our heads, no flashing lights, no increase of the pulse rates. We had really enjoyed very little in our marital relationship before the divorce. If we had been pressed for a comment, probably neither of us would have expressed love for the other. Yet, we began to understand that God wanted us to remarry. With very little emotion, I simply said to God one day, "Lord, if you want me to remarry Foy, I am willing to do so." Within hours after I made that commitment to Him, one of my greatest problems was staying out of Foy's bedroom. When I obeyed God and submitted my will to Him, He began to pour emotion (so-called "feelings") back into both Foy and me. It was through our obedience to Him that He began to place back into our anemic relationship all the emotions and attitudes which were necessary for the marriage to be a wholesome, healthy one. These emotions and attitudes were the blessings of His grace. He gave them to us because of our obedience to Him. God blesses obedience. He does not bless, and worse still, He withholds His blessings when we disobey. "If ye know these things, happy are ye if ye DO them" (emphasis mine), John 13:17 declares. Happiness is an emotion and it comes as a result of *doing* God's will as expressed in His written Word.

Can Love Be Defined?

Can love then in fact be defined? The great majority of the people, even Christians, with whom I have counseled have answered, "No." However, the Biblical concept of love can be defined and defined quite precisely. The thing which cannot be defined is the world's concept of love, which forces the word into the area of emotion. An emotion is very difficult to define. Biblical love is not an emotion. What then is the proper definition of love? Love, Biblical love, *agape'* love, is *an act of my will by which I give myself to the person of God's choosing once and for all, unconditionally.* "Show me the verse," you might quickly and properly request, as some folks have done. There is no one verse from which we derive this definition of love. There are many verses, however, which speak of love. When we apply the inductive method of extracting doctrinal truth from the verses, that is, drawing one Scriptural truth from a combination of several verses, we are rewarded with God's definition of love. Let's look at the definition carefully.

Agape love comes from God through an act of my will. When God commands me to love, that identifies love as a function of my will. God commands me to love. That means I can either obey Him or disobey Him. The choice is mine. By an act of my will, I choose. To love or not to love is my choice, hence it is a function of my will. As discovered earlier, the emotions come into prominence primarily after the choice, although they certainly are present to a degree before and during the making of that choice. With the intellect, of course, one thinks through several possible choices, but the final act of love is necessarily one of the will.

The second part of the definition states that one must "give himself" to another person. "For God so loved the world that He GAVE His only begotten Son . . . ." (John 3:16, emphasis mine) That love is a gift shows perhaps its most noteworthy characteristic. Love exists when you give freely, not when you demand or expect something in return. Notice, I avoided using the word "want," but wrote instead, "demand or expect." Love may "want" a like response but it will not demand nor expect it, else it fails to qualify as God's kind of love. Paul hones that thought to a fine edge in 1 Corinthians 7:4 when he wrote, "The wife hath not power (authority) of her own body, but the husband (does): and likewise also the husband hath not power (authority) of his own body, but the wife (does)" (parenthesis mine). How much clearer need God make it? Each marriage partner actually has control, perhaps even owner-ship, over the body of the other. What startling words those must have been to the first century readers, that a woman has authority over her husband's body. Although the verse refers directly to sex, the principle probably carries through into other areas of life. At the very least, the concept of cross-ownership is taught in the area of sex. We must give ourselves unconditionally to our marriage partner if we are to be obedient to our Lord.

We must, however, give ourselves to the person of God's choosing, not our own. If you are already married, you have the person of God's choosing. He or she might not have been His first choice for you, but once the marriage took place, God stamped (as it were) "married" on the "marriage license" of your souls. That person became your mate and he or she is the one to whom you are to give yourself.

If, however, you are not married and you plan to marry, make certain that you marry God's choice, not your own. Because this endeavor is not for the purpose of teaching you how you can know God's will for your life, that subject will not be explored in depth here. However, since the issue of one mar-rying God's choice rather than his or her own was raised, it seems to be proper to at least mention the three elements in discovering God's will. First, do the Scriptures allow you to marry the person? In other words, is the person a Christian? Secondly, after much prayer and perhaps fasting, has the Holy Spirit given you peace about marrying him or her? Thirdly, will the providential circumstances allow you to marry him or her? In other words, is the other person willing, has God clearly called both of you into complementary ministries, etc. If these three questions can be answered in the affirmative, then you should marry the person. If, however, even one is missing, then you should not marry, for the present time at least.

To continue, you ought to give yourself to your marriage partner "once for all." That is, you are not to give yourself to your mate temporarily. Make the decision final. Burn the bridges behind you and don't think what "might have been" with someone else. The gift is final, not a half-hearted one. One of the major notions which seems to be present in the minds of many young married couples today goes something like this, "If the marriage doesn't work out we can always get a divorce." May I suggest that with that kind of an attitude the marriage is already well on the road to failure. The gift of yourself to the other person is a final one, if true love is to be present in your marriage.

Finally, the gift of yourself to the other person is unconditional. That means that you should neither ask, demand, nor expect anything in return. A "gift" fails to qualify as a gift if a response is demanded. It becomes a sale. There were no conditions attached to the gift of the Son Jesus by the Father. God made no demands upon the world when He sent His Son. In love He sent Him. He didn't say, "World, you are lost, dying, undone, and doomed to hell. Now if you will treat My Son well, and accept Him, join a church and give your money, THEN I will give My Son to you to save you from your sins." To be sure, God would have been very pleased had the world so responded; but the world did not so respond. God sent His Son anyway, knowing full well the horror which lay before Him. That is love. That kind of love finds it easy to turn the other cheek. That kind of love perseveres. Husbands, we are to love our wives just that way.

The world in which we live knows little of that kind of love. Each marriage partner seems not only to expect a response out of the other person but even demands one and then calls the demand love. First Corinthians 13 gives to Christians clear characteristics of love. Nowhere in that entire chapter does love make a demand.

Husbands Don't Understand

In the beginning of this chapter I wrote, "I believe that the great preponderance of problems found in the beginning of most marriage breakdowns originate with the husband." May I now explain what I meant?

For a marriage to work, the husband must love his wife "even as Christ also loved the church and gave Himself for it." Husbands, you might retort,

"Doesn't God command the wives to love us the same way?" No, as a matter of fact He doesn't. Oh, in Titus 2:4, the apostle Paul writes to older women, "That they may teach the young women to be sober, to love their husbands, to love their children." The word "love" as used in Titus 2:4 isn't the word *"agape."* It is a weaker word, *phileo,* which conveys a type of friendship commitment. Why doesn't God command the wives to love (with *agape* love) their husbands? Remember chapter three? God doesn't command the wives to respond to the husbands because there is no need for the command. He built that response into the wife so that she responds automatically when the husband responds to her. Responding to a responsive husband is natural for a wife. Every "normal" woman wants to give herself over to her husband, not because she is com- manded to do so, but rather by nature. I laughingly tell the ladies, "God left nothing to 'chance' with you, female uncertainty being as it is. He made sure you would respond to your husbands. He included it as a part of your nature." (Note: There is no such thing as chance with God. The term is used only to illustrate contrasts.)

Why then do I say that the great preponderance of problems which occur in the early part of most marriages are traceable to husbands? I believe that most husbands enter the marriage relationship with a gross mis-concept and complete misunderstand- ing of the word love. I believe that most men enter the marriage commitment on the basis of LUST, not love.

In our vocabularies Satan has very cleverly substituted God's precious word love in the place of lust. Lust is an ugly word and unusable, so love has seemingly taken its place even, regrettable though it may be, in the lives of Christians. The culture in which we live, the movies, the television shows, the popular music and the teachings of some secular psychiatrists and psychologists tell us essentially that if we lust physically and emotionally after one woman more than all others, we love her and we should marry her. How tragic! How far from God's precious word love. Marriages often fail because lust fails. Lust cannot last toward one person for more than a few years, much less for a lifetime.

Now, most new husbands, I suspect, aren't aware that that which they are experiencing for their bride may be lust. They most likely believe that it is love. After all, everyone else is living and laboring under the same assumption. For the most part no one has bothered to tell many young grooms the difference.

A "Typical" Marriage

Keeping in mind what was written in chapter three about the wife and "her desire shall be to thy husband," let us trace the early days, weeks, and months of a marriage. The woman, filled with a desire to give herself to her new husband, and the man, armed with lust (which he mistakenly calls love), marry. It's exciting. The honeymoon, though, always ends and the young couple settles down to

begin the life of marriage. It's great, in the beginning. The young wife is busy making a home for her
husband, learning how to cook, enthusiastically
waiting for him to come home after work, just
wanting to be with him, to love him, to share her life
with him, to make him happy. The young husband is
anxious to get home after work to see his wife.
Coming home, he might pick his wife up, swing her
around, kiss her and lovingly demand to know
everything she has done throughout the day. He
willingly bestows great affection and much attention
upon her. He may offer to take her out to dinner so
she won't have to cook. He will probably open the
door for her to get into the car. He'll pull the chair
out for her to sit in the restaurant. Behold, he will
most likely even hold her hand in public. Why does
he do all these things? Probably for two reasons. He
knows she likes it. Secondly, he's thinking about
when they get home, bedtime. Oh, he probably isn't
conscious of all that. If he were asked about his
motives for giving his wife all that attention, he
might reply, "It's because I love her." Sadly, in his
mind that desire for his wife has been labeled
"love." "I love her," he says. The desire for her is a
powerful force in a man's life. For a short while it is
usually an all-consuming force, influencing every
part of the man's relationship with his wife.

Time passes. Something happens, something
most husbands never dream will happen. As the
mystique of the female anatomy begins to wane; as
the new becomes the old; when the unfamiliar
becomes the familiar, then lust begins to disappear

from him. As goes lust, so goes attention, and so goes time spent with the wife.

When lust begins to fade, the wife begins to notice that the attention and concern of the husband for her and her welfare is decreasing. In her sensitivity, the wife is conscious of the change. Remember the condemnation of Eve? The wife is supersensitive about everything that her husband does. Even though the husband might rationalize the "normalcy" of his decreased attention to his wife (it happens to everyone, he might suppose) and may not be conscious that his wife is aware of it, she *is* aware of it. Built into her nature is a sensitivity which makes her aware of it. The fact that her husband might now come in after work and flop down on the couch and yell, "When will dinner be ready?" bothers her. The difference in his actions and attitudes now, while they might appear insignificant to the husband, are very significant to the wife. As the intimate times between them decrease both in number and in intensity, she may begin to wonder, "What is wrong? Is it me? Is there someone else? What is happening?" Her mind begins to play tricks on her. She might even begin to question her husband about it, an action often labeled by him as nagging. The sad thing about the husband at this time is that he usually doesn't understand what is happening to him either. He just knows that those exciting drives and desires which motivated him so greatly in the beginning of the relationship no longer exist. He's probably a little confused and bewildered because those desires gave him the impetus he needed to get through the day's work; something to look forward to; something that filled that emptiness about his life which we examined in chapter two. He almost certainly doesn't want to lose it.

And so the drift apart continues, as it must. Lust for one person cannot usually continue. It will cease regardless of who or what the wife might be; regardless of how she looks; regardless of the sensuality of her actions. Consequently the wife's "antennae" get higher and higher.

If there is one area in the world in which the residents have proven that lust will dissipate, it's Hollywood. In Hollywood, as perhaps nowhere else, the women are beautiful, sensual, and divorced, in ever-increasing numbers.

As time continues to pass; as the familiarity with the female anatomy increases; and as the lust decreases, the husband and wife continue to drift apart. Eventually the actual sexual desire will decrease to a point where the man no longer views his loss of sex with his wife as all that tragic. This, of course, enhances his move away from her. He might no longer tell her how good she looks or take her out to dinner very often. He becomes embarrassed when she wants to hold his hand in public. He may oblige but it's usually to avoid an argument. The occasional sexual relationship satisfies him for a while. But apart from those times the husband may pay little serious attention to his wife. He may not want to talk to her, especially about serious matters. In fact, to find it necessary to talk to her may be annoying to him.

What about the wife? By now she is becoming increasingly disillusioned. She cannot understand the occurrences either. Because she is very sensitive to her husband's attitude and response toward her, she worries much of the time. The contrast between what her husband had been and what he appears to be now probably occupies the place of prominence in her mind. About this time several actions might create a negative spirit in her relationship to her husband. She might attempt to force her husband to explain the reason for his attitude and behavior. The husband, not really capable of explaining it, might become perturbed at the increased questioning. He refers to the questions as "nagging" and resents them. Frustration ensues, for perhaps nothing is quite as frustrating as trying to explain something you don't understand. It's much easier to grow annoyed and exclaim, "I don't know what's wrong," or "Nothing is wrong! What makes you think something is wrong?" At that response the wife's antennae rise higher; the questions continue; the worry increases. Arguments follow. Those occasional times when her husband responds to her for sexual satisfaction, while in one sense may be welcome, do little to satisfy her. Because her entire nature is geared for a total emotional relationship with her husband, sexual involvement fails to alleviate the worry. She quickly learns that after the sexual attention has ended, her husband usually falls into the same old patterns. All her other "wants" have yet to be met. Not only that, now she may begin to believe (commonly called "feel") she is being used sexually. This aggravates the problem for her, because most women resent being used by their husbands for sexual gratification. Therefore, the occasional sexual relationship may ultimately produce detrimental results. Believing she is being used, the woman may grow caustic and critical in her speech, and she may begin to withhold sex from her husband, using it as a weapon against him. The wife might now also begin to let herself go physically. She more than likely becomes somewhat depressed. She begins to neglect her appearance, possibly reasoning that "since he doesn't care anyway, I won't care either."

The husband, wondering himself what is happening and obviously aware that his wife is nagging, withholding sex, and not keeping herself cosmetically, now might begin to be increasingly aware of other women. He may notice those same exciting desires he once had for his wife awakening in him toward them. As the desire, lust if you will, decreases for his wife, the husband often begins to think, "I'm falling out of love with her." If he meets one woman in particular who produces more desire in him than others, he might begin to play with the idea that he is "falling in love" or at least "could fall in love" with her. Toying with this idea in his mind is pleasant, and it takes his mind off his problem with his wife. The day might come, and in our culture usually does, when the thought of a sexual relationship evolves into the real thing. Immorality is born into his life.

Even though the wife may not know that immorality is actually happening, she may begin to grow very suspicious. There may be traces of "evidence" on his clothing. He may begin to stay out late at night, drink heavily, and become increasingly interested in pornographic literature. All these things, added to his disinterest in her, combine to alert her. Tension deepens between them, arguments increase. The husband's lust for his wife may stop almost altogether. I have known men who lost all desire for intimacy with their wives. Nothing extinguishes lust quite as quickly as a nagging wife.

The husband might occasionally bring up the subject of divorce to his wife, toying with it in his mind. Or his wife may bring it up. Talk about divorce usually does begin though, gradually at first, then more seriously. The fact that children might have been born into the family, while both the husband and wife claim to be concerned about their welfare, usually appears to matter very little. Prides have been hurt, egos damaged, positions established, children forgotten.

The wife considers divorce as an answer because the husband doesn't respond to her, because he is not meeting her needs (which really may be only "wants"), and possibly because he is seeing another woman, if that sin in fact is occurring.

The husband usually honestly believes that he has "fallen out of love" with his wife and "fallen into love" with someone else. He may not really want the divorce. This may also be true with the wife, who like him may not want the divorce. But the culture in which we live says to a man and to a woman, "If you don't love your marriage partner and if you fall in love with someone else, you are excused to divorce and to marry the one you love." Many times that is precisely what happens. Through the misunderstanding of a word, Satan has won another victory. Divorce or misery! Those are the only two choices of which many couples are aware. A home destroyed and children damaged beyond most adults' ability to comprehend, partly because of one little word, love, and the blindness of many couples who never know that there is another choice.

The Answers

What is the answer, or answers? First, no reason for Christian couples to divorce ought ever exist. Of all people upon the face of the earth, Christians should understand God's meaning of love. The marriage ought to be built upon real love, not lust.

Secondly, we who counsel, teach, and preach the Word of God must ourselves understand, and we must convey to the woman, why she responds and reacts the way she does. She should understand that while the "super-sensitive characteristic" toward her husband might be present, it shouldn't be life-controlling. In Christ, she gains a great deal of dominion over those "jealous emotions." We must also teach the difference between lust and love and make as certain as humanly possible that both the man and woman know the difference. Marriage really shouldn't occur until both can explain the difference and promise to live according to it.

Thirdly, both the husband and wife must realize that God created them differently. They have different emotional makeup, different ways of doing things, different attitudes and actions.

Fourthly, Christ should be the center of every marriage. His will should be obeyed in all things. I really can't explain how a husband and wife can continue happily in a marriage relationship without Him. Frankly, not many do. In the culture in which we live, divorce is a way of life. We are told, "If you are not happy get a divorce."

Conclusion

Again, permit me to say that in the tracing of a relationship, a "behavioral skeleton" was presented. The events will vary from person to person, of course. Occasionally a couple will come for counsel who will say, "Not much of that happened to us." Quite frequently a couple will say, "Most of that happened to us." Every bit of it happened to Foy and me.

I want to conclude this chapter with a couple of comments. When the wife finally gives up on her husband and begins to turn from him toward some other man, the family is usually in big trouble. A woman can't normally move in and out of a relationship like a man can. When she gives up on the husband, usually only God can bring her back into the relationship. The man does not behave that way. Most men can zip in and out of their wives' bedrooms without much emotional involvement. But a woman moves more slowly into and more slowly out of a relationship, especially a physical one.

When a wife does begin to turn her "antennae" toward some other man, woe unto the husband who discovers it. He may have treated her like "dirt" and broken his marriage vows through immorality many times, but a man whose ego has been trampled by an unfaithful wife is a "picture to behold." "How could she do this to me?" he cries. How? Because God made her to give herself completely to a man. If Christ controls her, she has the power to endure an unloving husband. If not, she doesn't. "Husbands, love your wives even as Christ also loved the church and gave Himself for it," and most likely the counselor will never see you enter the door of his office.

IV APPLICATION

1 Men, write out the definition of love given to you by society. Can you do it? If you cannot, why not?

2 To illustrate how the meanings of words are altered through time, check the following words in your King James translation: *meet*, Genesis 2:18; *certify*, 2 Samuel 15:28; *ready*, Ezra 7:6; *straitened*, Job 37:10; *kine*, Amos 4:1; *waxed*, Matthew 13:15; *occupy*, Luke 19:13; *quit*, 1 Corinthians 16:13; *husband-man*, 2 Timothy 2:6; *prating*, 3 John 10.

3 Husbands, restudy the Biblical definition of love as given in this chapter. Have you called love a feeling or emotion? Do you agree now that that was wrong? How are the two definitions different?

4 Husbands, how did you choose your wife? Did you seek God's will and follow it or did you respond to an emotional surge toward her?

5 How did Issac choose Rebecca? How does the Biblical definition of love teach us to choose a mate?

6 Has God, in His Word, ever commanded you to do something which you did not want to do? Did you do it? What were the results of your action?

7 Do you, husband, still love your wife as much today as you did when you married her? By the world's definition? By God's?

8 Who owns your body? Intellectually, you know, God said your marriage mate does, but who REALLY does? Who controls it? What do you think would happen in your relationship if you were to truly give yourself to your mate?

9 List the ways in which your relationship to your wife (or husband) is conditional. Does your wife's response to you control your attitude and response toward her? Should it?

10 Husbands, are you as excited about being with your wife now as you were in the early days of your marriage? Why or why not?

11 Men, how long has it been since you told your wife "I love you" at a time when there was no way to accuse you of saying it for sexual purposes, like on the way out of the house going to work? Why not start doing that?

V

UPON WHOM SHOULD YOU BUILD YOUR LIFE?

A Grave Error

For whatever it is worth at the "market place" (probably nothing), I believe that many evangelical preachers and teachers have made in the past, and are even yet making, one of the gravest errors ever commited in the Christian church. I believe we are producing churches full of women, as well as men, who know very little about the true character of Biblical submission. I am, of course, speaking of the wife and her role in relation to her husband, although the error probably extends into other areas of life both in and out of the church. While these men of God earnestly preach the concept of submission, they often fail to define or explain the extent of it.

Submission—The Concept

Before explaining the above paragraph, may I say this about submission? It is a Biblical word which, of course, indicates that it is a Biblical doctrine (teaching). Scriptural submission pleases God, thus to refuse to submit to those whom God has granted authority over us is sin. God seems to have chosen the system of submissiveness to authority as His "modus operandi" for maintaining order among His creation. For example, all of us are to submit to the governmental authority over us (Romans 13:1-2; Titus 3:1; 1 Peter 2:13-14.) To refuse to do so when the law of government does not conflict with the law of God is rebellion and sin. Rebellion's final resting place is anarchy.

In addition, a chain of command exists within the church to which, according to God's Word, each member must submit (1 Thessalonians 5:12; Hebrews 13:17). Again, to refuse to submit to the church leaders whom God has placed over you is sin. By the way, Scripture knows nothing of a democratic form of church government. I wonder whether consciously or unconsciously, if the idea of democracy has become the "god" of some Americans. Several years ago now I listened to a famous radio and television preacher, a man of God, declare that many Americans, he believed, "were worshiping the god of liberty and freedom." At the time, the statement was suspect. I wonder now, however, if his statement might not warrant our consideration. Christ did not come into this world to establish democratic government. Praise the Lord that He has allowed us to live in one, but a democratic government too is only temporal and not deserving of our worship. Jesus came to free men from sin, Satan, death, and themselves, in order that we might become slaves to Him. When He establishes His millennial government upon the earth, it will not be a democratic one. Neither will the government of Heaven be democratic. God will own complete control. If you fear the idea of living where one Person has absolute authority, you may not enjoy Heaven. In the meantime, while we are on this side of Heaven we are to submit, not only to governmental authority, but also to church authority.

The Bible teaches yet another authority/submission relationship: the employer/employee. The employee, God teaches, is to submit to his employer (Ephesians 6:5-8; 1 Peter 2:18; Colossians 3:22-23). That seems to be a strange teaching in modern America, doesn't it? Whatever happened to this part of the Word of God?

In July and August of 1978, an illegal strike was called by the firefighters of Memphis, Tennessee, my hometown. Even though the strike was illegal, many Christians struck. A few did not. Threats were made against these non-striking firemen; against their homes; and against their families. One Christian fireman, an acquaintance though not a member of my particular church at that time was the only non-striking fireman in that particular firehouse. One day he telephoned me, requesting that I come to the firehouse for Bible study and prayer. When I got there the picket line was formed. I walked into the building unmolested and had prayer and Bible study with this brother, assuring him that his staying on the job in no way violated God's Word. He needed to know that, because his striking friends were hurling all kinds of threats and abuse at him. By the power of God he endured it. The exciting conclusion to the episode is that when the strike was settled, practically every co-fireman, including those who had threatened him, expressed admiration for his courageous stand. (The Christian friend had informed the strikers that the Word of God prohibited him from striking.) What a testimony! What a need in our time: Men and women who will stand with Jesus, regardless of the consequences! It wasn't easy for this dear brother to stand alone, but then standing with Jesus upon His Word has never been easy in any generation. The Word of God clearly teaches that we must submit to our employer's authority.

God also demands that children obey their parents. "Obeying" is the same as "submitting to" their authority (Ephesians 6:1-3; Colossians 3:20). Although this chapter does not provide the place for examining the condition of this command among Christians today, it ought to be said that perhaps few Scriptural commands are so flagrantly violated. Youthful rebellion toward parents cannot stand under the convicting gaze of Scripture. Neither can parents' almost lackadaisical and hopeless attitudes toward it. Both groups seem to ignore the Word of God in seeking solutions to the problem.

Finally, the Bible teaches that the wife is to submit to the authority of the husband (Ephesians 5:22-24; Colossians 3:18; 1 Peter 3:1-6). What is submission? To ask it another way, what does the

Bible mean when it says that a person is to submit to an authority? What does one surrender when he submits?

Submission—What Is It?

That question has been put to me many times in counseling sessions. I often listen with great interest and sometimes downright awe at some of the answers bouncing around evangelical hallways and flowing from conservative podiums and pupits.

Does that sound critical to you? I really hope it doesn't, because no hostility resides in my heart as I say it. Someone long ago said, "Christians should be able to disagree without being disagreeable." As I search my heart, I really believe that the things I am about to write, although different perhaps, are written in love, for I am about to examine certain popular interpretations of the concept of submission. Then, by our Lord's grace, I hope to present what to me the Bible teaches about the issue.

A—Submission

One view, the liberal one, simply denies the Biblical concept of submission. Some adherents to the liberal position might simply say that submission is no longer necessary. It might have been important, even necessary, years ago, but things have changed now, they declare. Because men and women will no longer stand for the idea to be imposed upon them, we ought to just drop it, they teach. Along with other Biblical teachings the doctrine of submission isn't relevant to twentieth-century man, these folks maintain. Thus, this view could be labeled "a-submission," that is, no-submission.

Situational Ethics Submission

Another view of submission expresses itself thusly: "Submission is good sometimes and it is bad sometimes, depending upon the situation." I refer to this teaching as the "situational ethics" view of submission. The situation determines whether or not one should submit. If a woman has a wonderful husband who treats her with dignity and respect, then she ought to submit to him. If, however, she marries a drunkard who curses her and beats the children, he doesn't deserve his wife's submission, therefore it may be acceptable for her not to submit to him. Whether or not something is right depends, for the promoters of this view, upon the situation, not upon the "absolute" of God's Word.

Partial Submission

The third teaching of submission I will call the "partial-submission, creative alternative" view. For the most part, this concept emanates primarily from conservative Christians. Simply stated, it commands us to submit to a higher authority "regardless." When we are ordered to do things which are contrary to Scripture, God will usually give us a creative alternative. If a husband, for example, commands his wife to engage in wife-swapping, obviously a sin, God will probably give to her a "creative alternative," meaning another course of action which is not sinful, but which satisfies the abnormal and sinful desires of her husband. Of course, God certainly can grant "creative alternatives" as He did with Daniel (Daniel chapter 1). But frankly I know of no place in Scripture where He promises to reward me with a creative alternative every time I face trials. Because He has done so with some men does not insure that He will do it with all men. As a matter of fact, God assures that ". . . all that will live godly in Christ Jesus shall suffer persecution." (2 Timothy 3:12) God promises to deliver us through suffering, not from it.

An attractive young wife came for counsel. She was a commited Christian, loving and serving her Lord and her husband. Her husband was not a Christian and he demanded of her a certain sexual act, an act clearly prohibited by Scripture. She, of course, wanted a creative alternative and prayed for one. Nothing else, however, would satisfy her sensual husband, so she took her stand—with Jesus. Verbal abuse and even some light physical abuse ensued, as did mental abuse. For months in love she suffered it and endured it. Finally the husband gave her an ultimatum; "Do it or divorce," he threatened. With tears in her eyes and love in her heart, she replied, "If you must divorce me, go ahead. I won't disobey my Lord." Eventually her husband, influenced and impressed by her stand, invited Jesus

Christ into his life. God's purpose often rises higher than a creative alternative. He wanted to manifest the power of Christian conviction through a small, inconsequential, commited housewife. A creative alternative would have denied to her the privilege to be so used by God.

Christ too sought for a creative alternative. In the Garden He prayed, " ... Father, all things are possible unto thee; take away this cup from me: nevertheless not what I will, but what thou wilt." (Mark 14:36) Our Lord must have been asking God if there was some other way, an alternate way, by which sin could be taken from men so that He would not have to suffer the legal guilt for it. We know that no other way ever came, for indeed Jesus willingly endured precisely what He had momentarily requested that He not be made to do, i.e., "take away this cup (of suffering) from me" (parenthesis mine).

Even as I write these things, I ask not to be misunderstood. Please allow me to say once again that as I examine my heart before the Lord, I find no animosity nor bitterness. I write in love and appreciation for God's great servants who teach the concept of "creative alternatives." Man, though, is never our final authority. God's Word must continue to be our final authority.

Total Submission

Another view of submission, taught occasionally, insists that wives, in particular, must submit to

their husbands in everything, even sin. This doctrine might be labeled the "total submission" view.
"Do people really teach that?" you might ask. Yes,
some people really do. It probably isn't widely
taught, but it deserves a comment because of its
destructive nature when it is taught. Do you understand the error(s) in it? First, it allows sin to be
acceptable in certain situations (which is almost a
"back-door" version of situational submission),
something the Word of God does not do. Secondly,
it establishes the husband as the Christian wife's
final authority, also something the Bible never does.
A woman's final authority is the same as a man's—
the Word of God. She, like her husband, should
never deliberately break God's law, no matter who
commands it.

Biblical Submission

What then does the Word of God teach regard-
ing a wife's relationship to her husband? The first
verse is found in Genesis 3:16, a verse which we
examined in chapter two, ". . . and he (husband)
shall rule over thee." Other well-known verses are
found in Ephesians, Colossians and First Peter, as
mentioned earlier. After admonishing the Christians of Ephesus to begin "Submitting yourselves
one to another in the fear of God" (Ephesians 5:21),
Paul turns his attention to the wives of that church.
"Wives, submit yourselves unto your own husbands,
as unto the Lord. For the husband is the head of the
wife, even as Christ is the head of the church: and

he is the Savior of the body. Therefore as the church
is subject unto Christ, so let the wives be to their
own husbands in every thing." (Ephesian 5:22-24)
Paul reminds the Colossians of the same thing in
Colossians 3:18. "Wives, submit yourselves unto
your own husbands, as it is fit in the Lord."

That the Word of God instructs a wife to submit
to her husband cannot be questioned. The Bible
teaches submission. The question and consequently the problem arises though, not so much in the
meaning of the word submit as in the extent of it.
The meaning of the word could hardly be misunderstood. According to the American Everyday
Dictionary, it means, "to yield in surrender, compli-
ance, or obedience; to refer to the judgment of
another; to state or urge with deference."

Now, let's refer back to the very first paragraph
of this chapter where I wrote, "I believe that
evangelical preachers and teachers have made in
the past, and are even yet making, one of the
gravest errors ever commited in the Christian
church." I meant simply this: When we preachers
and teachers stand before the people and command the wives to submit to their husbands without
explaining the extent of that submission, we might
be encouraging the women to do something that
God prohibits in His Word. At the very least, we are
not warning them against doing something wrong.
The wife's nature is to "desire her husband." She
possesses a natural tendency to submit to him, at
least to some degree. But she should never, never,
never submit her mind, her emotions, nor her

relationship with the Lord Jesus to her husband. She ought to submit to her husband totally in relation to WHAT SHE DOES in the family unit but she should never submit to him in relation to WHO SHE IS. Please allow me to explain the difference between the two, which unfortunately so many Christian leaders are failing to do.

When God gave to woman His Holy Spirit and a like intellect with man, He bestowed upon her the privilege of being co-king and co-priest with her husband. A wife's relationship with the Lord ought not noticeably suffer when her husband's relationship to Him isn't right. She isn't funneled into God's presence through her husband any more than she is compelled to enter into His presence through a priest or through the Virgin Mary. She owns direct access into God's presence just as any Christian man does. The Christian woman is every bit as precious to God as a man. She is a "co-heir of the grace of life" (1 Peter 3:7) with her husband, not a sub-heir. But by the time many Bible-believing teachers get through preaching on the subject of submission, the wife may have been denied that state, at least in her own mind. Unfortunately much teaching on the subject declares by silence that the wife should submit to her husband not only in "what she does" but in "who she is." In other words she isn't warned against building her entire life, physical, emotional, mental, and quite often spiritual, upon her husband. "As goes the husband so goes the wife." When he is happy, she is happy. When he is sad or mad, so is she. When he is in fellowship with the Lord, she is also, etc., etc. I strongly deny the existence of a Biblical basis for this position. I fail to discover where God ever intended for one of His children to be totally dependent, emotionally or spiritually, upon anyone or anything other than His dear Son, Jesus. To be that subservient, the wife cannot help but build her life upon her husband, a wrong foundation and one that quite often is shifting sand, as the divorce courts attest. Jesus ought to be every man's foundation, and He ought to be every woman's foundation.

The wife then ought to submit to her husband in relation to "what she does," but not in relation to "who she is." "But wait," you might reply, "how does that actually work? How can you make that division?" Permit me to partly answer the second question first. It will be fully examined later in this chapter. Meanwhile, before answering completely, I believe that there is a strong Biblical basis for making the division, because the Bible was written to Christian wives as well as to their saved husbands.

The first question is a significant one. How can a woman actually submit to her husband in relation to what she does but not in relation to who she is? May I illustrate the answer two ways? First, with the Trinity. When Jesus came into this world He submitted His will to His Father. He said more than once, "Not My will but Thine be done." (Matthew 26:39) The Holy Spirit came to direct men not to Himself, but to Jesus (John 16:14). Now in relation to the ministries of the Father, Son, and Holy Spirit, that is, what they did, there is within the Godhead an apparent chain of command. But in relation to Who the Persons of the Godhead are, there is full and absolute equality. God the Father, God the Son, and God the Holy Spirit are completely equal in every way in regard to their persons. One is as much God as the other, and as loving, righteous, eternal, omnipotent, etc. as the other. In regard to "Who they are" total equality exists, but in relation to what they do, there is a chain of command.

The second illustration might be discovered in any secular organization. The church certainly should project it. When I accepted the staff position at Broadway Church, I was expected to submit to the authority of my pastor. I have done that. I recognize him as my God-appointed authority. He serves over me in relation to what I do as a staff member of the church. The things I do must conform to Biblical, thus church, standards. But in relation to who I am, I suppose that God holds my life to be as precious as my pastor's. My life is certainly as valuable before the state law as my pastor's. Everything being equal, if two murderers came into the church and killed both the pastor and me, one killing him, the other murdering me, is the pastor's life before the law any more valuable than mine simply because he holds a position of authority over me? Again, everything being equal, no mitigating circumstances, etc., when these two men appear for sentencing, my pastor's murderer would not receive greater condemnation than the one who killed me, even though in authority the pastor was my superior.

A Real Difference

With these two illustrations we can understand the very real difference between submitting in relation to "what we do" as opposed to "who we are." The woman's submission should be total in regard to "what she does" as wife to her husband and mother to his children, but restricted in relation to "who she is." The woman should understand that God will judge her husband for every decision the family makes. The role of the wife, however, in family decision-making should be an important one. She ought to strive very diligently, as a committee of one, to aid her husband in making right decisions. Her role demands it. She has been given to her husband as a "help-mate" (Genesis 2:18). Notice those two words. She is a helper. That means that she is to help her husband. A loving, conscientious wife knows that God will hold her husband accountable for the actions and spiritual atmosphere of his family. She ought to strive, therefore, to make him successful in both areas. She should in love offer suggestions, make comments, think through possible courses of action, and encourage her husband. She ought to warn him lovingly when he is making the wrong choice. She should provide her husband with "thought-through" proposals about family decisions. But she must never argue with him about the final decision. The final decision must be the husband's. A wise husband will utilize his "help-mate" and seriously consider her suggestions, but the family's final course of action should be charted by the husband. Before God, he stands responsible for it. A Christian wife should understand that God will not judge her accountable for a wrong family decision even when that decision was a result of her suggestion. God holds the husband responsible for family matters regardless of who contributed the idea or ideas. A Godly wife will yield to that fact rather than demand the right to make the final decision, which, if wrong, carries no divine chastisement.

Not only does Scripture ordain the wife to be a helper but it also calls her a mate. You are probably at this moment wearing two shoes. They are mates, or should be. Is either shoe more precious, more valuable, or more important than the other? Wife, you are a mate to your husband. You are not a subperson who is to help, nor a mate to dominate. You are equal in every way as to your person (Galatians 3:28). Your role as mate summons you to help your husband make right choices and to be successful before God.

Few Understand

God has honored me with many opportunities to counsel people. Usually I see fifty to eighty people per month. Probably eighty-five percent of my counselees are women. Very few of these precious ladies understand the Biblical concept of submission. Most of them realize that something is amiss in this area, but when they submit as they understand it, they often find it difficult to maintain their own emotional stability. If they fail to submit at all, marital conflict occurs. What a freedom for most of them to learn that even though they must submit in relation to what they do in the family, they are not required to be emotionally dependent upon their husbands! A majority are perfectly willing to submit, but not understanding the difference between submission in "doing" as opposed to submitting in "being," they often grow discouraged as they try to maintain their own emotional lives, which are so often dependent upon their husband's emotional state.

An Eternal Foundation

Earlier I suggested that a question might be asked, "How can you make this division, that is, between submitting in 'doing' and submitting in 'being?'" I believe that there is a strong Biblical basis for drawing the distinction between these two concepts. Unless the Bible was written only for men (and it was not), it seems to teach that every Christian ought to build his or her life upon the foundation of our Lord, not upon temporal things. Four verifying Scripture verses have been chosen from many which speak on the subject.

Isaiah 26:3 says, "Thou wilt keep him in perfect peace, whose mind is stayed on thee. . . ." Peace is a much-sought-after luxury these days. Nations and individuals who indwell these nations want and are seeking peace. Peace, we Christians believe, comes only from God. God provides for His own children two levels of peace. At the moment of conversion, we inherit peace WITH God. The warfare ends between God and us; the armistice is signed; and God and man are on the same side. But even though we may have peace with God, we may still lack the "day-by-day" peace OF God in our lives. That kind of peace comes from living a life characterized by obedience to God's Word, the Bible.

The application of the verse as it relates to the subject of this chapter is that for a child of God, peace does not come from our relationship to temporal things. It comes to us as we allow God to furnish the purpose for our lives. That appears to be the meaning of the verb "stayed." Our minds, thoughts, and purposes need to be controlled by God, not by people, things, or situations. Again, provided this verse does not apply only to men, God here seems to be guiding women into a dependent relationship with Him. A wife's mind should be "stayed" on God. Her steadfast purpose ought to be to depend upon God, not upon her husband, children, home, social position, nor any temporal thing.

In teaching about Christian suffering, the apostle Paul comments, "While we look not at the things which are seen, but at the things which are not seen: for the things which are seen are temporal; but the things which are not seen are eternal." (2 Corinthians 4:18) The context of the verse, as I mentioned before, deals with suffering but the verse itself provides for us an important concept in regard to what should be the focal point of our lives.

We are not to "look at" things which can be seen. Obviously Paul isn't considering physical eyesight. We must "look at" physical things just to live safely through the day. Paul probably intends for all of us, husbands and wives alike, to "depend" upon, not visible things, but unseen things. Paul reasons that the "seen" things are but temporary. The unseen things are eternal. What are the eternal things to which the apostle refers? It seems to me that he is exhorting men and women to depend upon, that is to build their lives upon, God, the Lord Jesus Christ and His work and upon His Word. These things are to provide the foundation for our lives, not the shifting sand of temporary things (Matthew 7:26).

Your Marriage Will End

Wives, whether or not you have ever realized it, marriage is a temporal thing. Your marriage will end. Hopefully, death or our Lord's return will be that which concludes it. More than fifty percent of the marriages in this country, though, are finalized before death, through divorce. Either way, the marriage will end. Should you build your life upon a man or a marriage when both are temporal? Many women have done it. When, therefore, the marriage ends, the wife's reason for existence ends. God, it seems to me, never intended for His children, whether they be male or female, to be controlled by things so temporal. Wives, submit the things which you do in your family to the authority of your husbands, but build your reason to exist upon your relationship with Jesus. That will not make you a less-devoted wife. It will cause you to be a superior one. When Scripture controls your relationship to your husband, you will be successful as a wife. Your success, therefore, won't be measured by your husband's response to you, but rather it will be determined by your obedience to God, as it is in all other areas of life.

The third verse of Scripture is Colossians 3:2. It reads, "Set your affection on things above, not on things on the earth." Here God, speaking through Paul, issues a command: Let your mind (affection) be controlled by God, not by earthly things. How much clearer could it be? Wives, this verse was likewise written to you as well as to your husbands. God isn't asking you nor pleading with you. He is commanding you as His child, risen with Christ, indwelt by His Holy Spirit, as one who will return in triumph with Him at the end-time, to look into Heaven to find your reason for living. Your mind, affection, emotions are to be controlled by Jesus, not the things on this earth.

Finally, in Hebrews God through the human writer exhorts, "Looking unto Jesus the author and finisher of our faith; who for the joy that was set before him endured the cross, despising the shame, and is set down at the right hand of the throne of God." (Hebrews 12:2) Once again, God writes to every Christian. He says literally that you are to rivet your gaze upon Jesus. That is, look to Him for your motivation for life, your purpose for existing, and your expectations for the future. Once again permit me to say that this verse pertains to wives as well as husbands, single folks and children. All Christians should depend upon Him.

Many woman have come and are coming into my office who haven't heeded these verses. They have built their hopes, expectations, dreams and purposes upon a man and upon a marriage. When that man fails his wife; when he begins to drift away from her; when he finally (in some cases) sins against her and against God; when he leaves and divorces her or when he dies, her whole world then collapses. She built her life upon the wrong foundation, one which is temporal.

Build Your Life Upon Him

Ladies, build your lives upon Jesus. You need not build your lives upon your husbands in order to be good, loyal, submitting wives. As I mentioned before, just the opposite is true. A good, loyal, submitting wife doesn't demand from a husband that which should only be expected from God. A good, loyal, submitting wife looks to the Author and Finisher of her faith. She builds her life upon the solid foundation of her relationship with Him, not upon the uncertainty of temporal things. I don't believe that wives will ever know the deep joy and constant peace of God until they do. Ladies, fear of losing that upon which you have built the purpose for your existence will tend to dominate your mind, thus it will tend to control your life. But when you build your life upon the One Who is the same yesterday, today, and forever, the loss of everything else, while it might hurt, will not destroy you.

The same concept, of course, is also true for men. In our culture, it isn't quite as common for a man to build his life upon his wife, at least not after the first year or so of marriage. However, it does happen occasionally. The answer remains constant for all of us, "Look to Jesus." That is, our relationship with Him ought to provide our purpose and hope for living.

A Personal Application

As the Lord is my witness, and He is of course, I believe that if Foy were to lose me through any means, her life would continue almost the same as it will with me. Tears would be present, of course; but a change in her lifestyle? No! Foy isn't building her life upon me. I believe the same thing about myself in the event that I lost her. My life would not drastically change, by our Lord's grace. "With this attitude," you might wonder, "can Foy still be submissive to him?" Adamantly, yes, in relation to what she does in fulfilling her role as a wife. Adamantly, no, in relation to her emotional state. I can affect her emotions. I cannot control them. Her emotional state depends mostly upon her relationship with Jesus, and He never changes.

V APPLICATION

1 Searching your heart, do you have trouble submitting to the authority over you? To the government? To your employer? To your parents? To other Christians (Ephesians 5:21)? To your husband?

2 To which of the above do you find it most difficult to submit? Why?

3 Has the one in authority over you ever ordered you to commit an unscriptural act? How did you handle it? How do you think you should have handled it?

4 Ladies, do you really believe God gave the Bible to you as well as to men? Men, do you? Why or why not?

5 Write out in your own words, your understanding of submission in relation to "doing" and in relation to "being."

6 What most often controls your emotional state? Is it your husband? Wife? Marriage? Employer? Child? Parents?

7 Looking back at question number 6, would you say that you are therefore building your life on the thing which controls your life? Should you be?

8 Can you right now, commit yourself to our Lord to build your life upon Him and submit yourself to His authority, and His appointed authority over you?

9 What, from the depths of your heart, is your reason for living? What should be?

VI

I'VE ALWAYS DONE IT THIS WAY! I CAN'T CHANGE

Introduction

Before discussing God's method of changing people, I want to give credit where it should be given. Much of the material in this chapter originated with Dr. Jay Adams, a noted teacher, counselor, and author of several books, including *Christian Counselor's Manual* published by Baker Book House in Grand Rapids, Michigan. Occasionally references to statements contained in that book will be made. His Biblical counseling concepts have been invaluable to me and I enthusiastically recommend all of his counseling works. Dr. Adam's books are excellent because they counsel with God's Word only, minus, of course, humanism and every other "ism."

"Creatures" of Habit

Did you know that you and I are " creatures" of habit? Some folks might loudly deny it; "Don't accuse me of that!" they cry. Being a creature of habit, however, is not necessarily bad. As Jay Adams teaches, habit is a marvelous gift from God. But like those who command, "Don't preach to me," as though preaching were some devious, sordid exercise of the devil, habit, too, often suffers condemnation. As a matter of fact both preaching and our habitual natures are Biblical, and both are given to us for our good, not our detriment. But wait! "How can habit be good?" you are probably wondering. May I answer that question by asking one? When you dressed this morning which arm did you put through your shirt or blouse first? Which arm did you put in first yesterday? Could you have put the same arm in first today that you put in first yesterday? You may have trouble even remembering. That is because you are not required to think about which arm you put in first in order to put on the shirt or blouse. You dressed by habit. The same thing could be said about putting on all your other "standard" clothes, brushing your teeth, sweeping the floor and hundreds of other "mundane" tasks and activities in which you are engaged throughout the day. You accomplish many of these things without ever thinking about doing them. You have done them so often that they have become "habits," or second nature to you.

What is the advantage of habit, that is, performing tasks without having to think about doing them? Simply this: Habit frees your mind to consider the more important activities of the day while you execute the ordinary ones. While you are dressing, for example, you may be considering which of the day's many tasks to do first, second, third, etc. While you are driving your car, your mind might be reflecting upon a business deal (although wisdom would prohibit a complete disregard of the fact that you are driving). While shaving or brushing your teeth, you could be formulating plans for the church social. The list and examples are endless, and probably by now the concept is relatively clear to you. Can you imagine life's complexity if you and I were forced to consider each movement of our bodies before executing it? Why, just walking across the room would demand concentration. "Now I must pick up my right leg, now my left leg, now my right leg, etc. . . ." Doubtless habit is one of God's most marvelous gifts to His human creation.

Habit—Not an Option

Habit is not an option! We are habitual creatures, whether we want to be or not. Our journeys through life are literally filled with habits. Once a habit forms, as you probably know, it becomes very difficult to break. We will discover later how that can be done, however. Meanwhile, since actions, reactions, attitudes and responses can and do become habits, God carefully commands us to form good ones. Jay Adams reminds us that 1 Timothy 4:7 commands, ". . . exercise thyself rather unto godliness." Dr. Adams points out that the original word which has been translated "exercise" is the transliterated word "gumnazo," from which the English language draws the words gymnastics and gymnasium. By using that particular word God commands us to train ourselves toward Godly living. The word seems to corral the idea that we can actually train ourselves so that Godly actions, reactions, attitudes and responses will become habit or second nature to us. This means that in the same way that we tie our shoe while our mind considers something else (because tying our shoe has become second nature), Godly actions, reactions, attitudes, and responses can be effected just as naturally, without our thinking about it.

"Paige, you mean to tell me," you might ask, "that doing something nice to someone who hates me and desires my hurt can become natural, or habit?" Yes, that is precisely what I am saying and it is just one more magnificent advantage in being a Christian. God has made available to us great power, enough to make a habit of loving those who hate us.

Rather than exercising ourselves to respond and react in a Godly manner, though, we often train ourselves, under the auspices of Satan and the world, to respond and react in kind. If someone strikes us, our society teaches that we may strike back. This kind of reaction is not God's way of responding, however. It leads inevitably to hatred and bitterness. If a husband is having an adulterous relationship with a woman, our society frees his wife to curse, condemn, hate, threaten, and finally to divorce him. That response leads to bitterness, hatred and a satanic slavery to one's own emotions.

God desires that no one hate nor become bitter. What a horrible life hatred produces! Where hatred and bitterness reside, there will be no joy nor peace. Without joy and peace life becomes a burden. God said, in contrast, "Exercise thyself rather unto godliness."

Exercise Yourself to Godliness

A man says, "Paige, that sounds good, but how do I train myself to stop yelling at my son when yelling at him has already become second nature, automatic, habit, with me?" A wife might likewise ask, "How do I stop nagging my husband after I have discovered he has commited adultery?" (Both of these questions, incidentally, have been asked me quite often.)

To answer, every person needs change in at least two areas of his life: his actions and his attitude. In the case of the man who yells at his son and the wife who nags her husband, both their attitudes and their actions need changing. The man's attitude toward his son needs to be one of love and patience rather than one of condemnation. His action toward his son needs to be one of firm, consistent correction with a soft voice. The wife of the adulterous husband needs an attitude and action change, too. She needs an attitude of trust rather than one of suspicion and she should speak to him in a soft voice as well as respond to him in other marital relationships. Like them, you and I need to have our attitudes and actions altered in certain areas of our lives (unless of course moral perfection has been obtained, which is highly unlikely). Now, how can that happen? How can you and I acquire an alteration in our attitude and actions?

Two Views to Change

Two basic views leading to desired changes in attitude and action exist. One is God's way, and it works. The other is the world's (and secular psychiatry's) way and it does not work.

Secular psychiatry says essentially that in order to derive a change in man's actions, his attitude must be altered by therapy, drugs, shock treatment, or a combination of these things. This concept insists that a man "does what he is," that his behavior is a direct product of his attitude. But, teaches secular psychiatry, his attitude was fashioned and controlled by his upbringing, his deprivation and/or abuses as a child, by the Victorian society which erroneously taught him that there were absolutes of right and wrong, by genetic inheritance, and by the environment. All these past influences and forces formed in man certain conflicts, which produced certain attitudes which caused his erratic behavior. Now obviously the desired thing, in order to effect change, would be to somehow reduce man back to the embryo stage, place him back into his mother's womb, allow him to be born again and reared with total and complete "freedom." This, it is believed, would produce a proper attitude, thereby locking the subject into proper behavior. The journey required to disprove that thesis is a short one. The first man, Adam certainly suffered none of the above so-called "wrongs," but it was through him that all erratic human behavior originated.

Obviously a person cannot be reduced back to the embryo stage and reinserted into his mother's womb. Therefore secular psychiatry insists that a change in his attitude through therapy, drugs, shock, etc., becomes his only hope. And so, as Jay Adams states, the secular psychiatrist "expert" is called into action with his drugs and his shock treatments. The psychiatrist's method of behavioral change then comprises altering a person's attitude. Change his attitude, they believe, and you will change his behavior. At best, it is a shot in the dark. At worst, long-range emotional and spiritual damage often occurs. In no case does it bring permanent and true change, at least not for the better.

God, even more than the secular psychiatrist, desires an attitude and behavioral change. But God seems to approach the problem from the opposite direction. Carefully consider the message of John 13:17: "If ye know these things, HAPPY are ye if ye DO them." Proverbs 29:18b repeats this truth by proclaiming "... he that keepeth the law, happy is he." Revelation 1:3 states, "Blessed (happiness multiplied) is he that readeth, and they that hear the words of this prophecy, and keep those things which are written therein. ..." (parenthesis mine). Happiness reflects a good attitude. Thus, a good attitude characterizes a happy man, and God says happiness comes through obedience to His law. Attitude, then, is directly affected, not by a self-appointed and humanist-trained "expert," but by obedience to God's Word. Obey Me and I'll bless you, disobey Me and I'll withhold My blessings, God warns many times in the Bible.

Actions Over Attitudes

God's method really does make sense. Of the two parts about me which need changing, my attitude and my actions (behavior), I have the ability to control only one of them, my actions. I cannot control my attitude or effect change in it. Therefore what God seems to be telling us is this: "My children, you change the part you can change and I'll change the part of you that you cannot change. You obey Me and through that obedience, I'll initiate a change in your attitude." Two examples exist in my own life by which I can illustrate these truths: whiskey and pecan pie.

Before I became a Christian, many of my friends and I drank lots of whiskey. One friend with whom I often drank was, I believe, an alcoholic (so called by the world but to whom the Bible refers as a drunkard). He drank every day, so far as I know. At least he drank every time we were together. I had not seen him, though, for several months following my conversion to Christ. After I became a Christian our trails parted. He continued in his direction; my path was reversed. About six months after Foy and I accepted Jesus, we attended an Ole Miss football game. Following the game, we waited for the traffic to clear out some before leaving. We were standing at the rear of our car "nibbling" on "goodies" which we had brought to the game when a car horn honked. Glancing around, I saw my old friend waving at me. He pulled his automobile over near us and stopped. On the seat next to him were two empty fifth whiskey bottles and his female companion. After the niceties of "How have you been," etc., had been expressed, my friend grew very solemn. He commented, "Paige, I've heard that you have been speaking in churches." I replied, "Yes." I was aware that like the old me, he had not been spending much time in churches. He continued, "I've talked to some folks who've heard you speak and they said that you said you quit drinking." I answered, "Yes, I would like to talk to you about that." Quickly he responded, "I don't want to talk to you about that. I've quit drinking lots of times. But, Paige," he continued, "some of these people told me that you said you quit *wanting* to drink. Now, that's what I want to talk to you about. I know you. How did you quit wanting to drink?" My friend probably never realized it but he asked a profound question, a question which has concerned and confounded men of all ages. Can you actually gain a change in inner desires and attitudes? I took the opportunity to share the Good News with this friend. "Through my obedience to the Savior," I told him, "God actually changed me from the inside out." He changed my desire for whiskey into an abhorrence. I could not alter my desire for the drink, but I could stop drinking it! I could obey God. God then accomplished the part I could not accomplish as I did the part which I could do.

The other example of this is pecan pie, my favorite dessert. I honestly believe I could eat it every meal. During my college football career, I would usually leave off sweets during the season. But on the Saturday of the last game, my mother would bake a pecan pie for me. After the game, I would buy a couple of milkshakes and eat the whole pie, enjoying every bite. It never did make me sick, though one might wonder why it didn't. I still like it.

Now, the question is, can I refrain from eating pecan pie? Yes! Can I make myself dislike pecan pie? No! You see, my attitude toward pecan pie is one of fondness. I really like it. My behavior toward it, however, can be one of abstinence. I don't have to eat it. I can control my *behavior* toward pecan pie, but I can't control my *attitude* toward it. If pecan pie graces the table I have the ability to reject it. I might be forced to excuse myself from the table and run out the door in order not to eat it, but I can do that. I might even be compelled to run a mile down the road to remove myself from the temptation. Even though, however, I have controlled my behavior and have refused to eat the pie, my desire for it hasn't changed, even if I sit under a juniper tree and pout, as Elijah did (1 Kings 19:4). I said all that to say again that you and I can control our behavior. What we cannot control are our attitudes or desires. Only God can alter attitudes, and He apparently only alters them through our behavioral obedience to Him.

I wonder how many of you like black coffee? How many of you who now like it, once drank it with cream or sugar or both? Now, how many of you liked black coffee the first time you drank it? What changed your attitude toward black coffee? By continuously drinking it black you probably grew first to tolerate it, then to endure it, and finally to enjoy it. Therefore through the process of "doing" you can actually "become" different, or have your attitude changed.

Train Yourself

The fact that we can change is perhaps best proven by a command of Scripture, as Jay Adams relates, and which we have examined before. First Timothy 4:7b commands, ". . . and exercise thyself rather unto godliness." Again, the word exercise is the Greek word "gumnazo." We derive our English words gymnastics and gymnasium from it. Do you see the significance of the word now? With it, God teaches that we can actually train ourselves to live Godly lives. God uses the word again in Hebrews 5:14 where we learn that we can exercise, or train, ourselves to discern between good and evil. It is used a third time in 2 Peter 2:14. Describing apostate preachers and teachers, Peter states, "Having eyes full of adultery, and that cannot cease from sin; beguiling unstable souls: an heart they have exercised with covetous practices . . . ." In all three instances the word forcefully teaches that man can actually train himself for Godly living; or to discern between good and evil; or to live an ungodly life. These truths are extremely important not only in spiritual "preventative maintenance" but also in moral "correction." That is, a person can train himself from childhood to live a Godly Christian life so that Christlike actions, attitudes, responses, and reactions might become "second nature" or habit to him. Or, in the event that he has trained himself in ungodly actions, attitudes, responses, and reactions, he can "de-train" himself in these things and "re-train" himself in the Godly way. The Scriptures call this process putting off and putting on.

Putting Off—Putting On

Paul writes in Ephesians 4:22-32:

That ye put off concerning the former conversation the old man, which is corrupt according to the deceitful lusts; And be renewed in the spirit of your mind; And that ye put on the new man, which after God is created in righteousness and true holiness. Wherefore putting away lying, speak every man truth with his neighbor: for we are members one of another. Be ye angry and sin not: let not the sun go down upon your wrath: Neither give place to the devil. Let him that stole steal no more: but rather let him labour, working with his hands the thing which is good, that he may have to give to him that needeth. Let no corrupt communication proceed out of your mouth, but that which is good to the use of edifying, that it may minister grace unto the hearers. And grieve not the Holy Spirit of God, whereby ye are sealed unto the day of redemption. Let all bitterness, and wrath, and anger, and clamour, and evil speaking, be put away from you, with all malice: And be ye kind one to another, tenderhearted, forgiving one another, even as God for Christ's sake hath forgiven you.

If you read the verses very carefully, you will notice that Paul used the words "put off" and "put on" several times, permeating the entire section of Scriptures with this principle. The passage teaches God's method of taking us from "where we are" to "where we ought to be," even though "where we are" might be an ungodly lifestyle, characterized by bad habits. Simply stated, God tells us to replace the old bad habit with a new good one. Not only, therefore, are we to stop doing the bad thing but we are to commence doing the good one. Through the "doing" of the good thing, shortly (Jay Adams says from six to eight weeks) the desire for the old bad habit will go away and the new good habit will take its place as "second nature."

Victory Over Desire

The above concept works, as has been proven many times in my own personal life. Even after I was converted, old evil desires would haunt me. The drinking and partying had become such an integral part of my pre-salvation lifestyle that even after I was saved there periodically surged into my mind desires for these things again. I soon learned how to saturate my mind with God's Word rather than indulging in sinful thought and/or behavior. It wasn't long before the old lifestyle had been completely replaced by the new one. As I obeyed God, studied His Word, and fled from temptation, I actually experienced a change in my desires or attitudes toward the former life. I "exercised" myself unto godliness, by His grace.

Change is the message of Ephesians 4. Paul says to put off the old way of life and put on the new righteous and holy one. How, Paul? He explains that we are to substitute truth-telling for lying. We can be angry but not with sin, that is, with spite and malice. We must put off stealing and put on working for a living. We are to put off evil-speaking and put on speaking that which is edifying. Finally, we are to put off bitterness, wrath, etc. and put on tender-heartedness, kindness, etc. In each case, we aren't only to *stop* doing that which is bad but we are to *start* doing that which is good. As the substitution continues, God begins to make the good thing more and more natural for us, eventually altering even our desire or attitude toward both the bad thing and the good thing. He will cause us to abhor the evil life and to like the good one.

Is That Hypocrisy?

"But wait," you might ask. "Isn't that hypocrisy? Won't doing something which is unnatural make me a hypocrite?" (Satan would have us think that.) Absolutely no human response, attitude, action, nor reaction ever becomes so evil that it cannot be corrected through the substitution of a Biblical alternative. In other words, the Scriptures establish God's way of responding, acting, reacting, and His desired attitude for all human situations. When I do what God has commanded me to do even though I might have desired to do just the opposite, I am being obedient to God. The existential society in which we live tells me that I am to do what I "feel" like doing, that is, what I want to do. To do otherwise, it falsely maintains, is to become hypocritical. God however teaches the reverse. He recognizes obedience as the highest calling of man. We are to obey whether we "feel like it" (want to) or not. Therefore when we obey God, we aren't sinning, even if we obey semi-unenthusiastically. When my bad attitude fashions bad behavior, I sin, but when I obey God, even with a faulty attitude, He uses my obedience to alter my attitude.

Let me illustrate with a hypothetical case. Suppose a man has grown very critical of his wife's negligence in properly caring for the home. She allows the children to leave their dirty clothes on the floor for days. The beds are almost never made. Dirty dishes constantly fill the sink and pollute the cabinets. The den floor seldom gets vacuumed, the kitchen floor has never shined, etc. The husband automatically (by habit) responds negatively as soon as he walks into the home and sees the mess. Perhaps because he has become a Christian or for some other reason, the husband wants to change his attitude toward his wife and her sloppy housekeeping. How can he do it?

First, he must come to realize, as he probably has, that his reactions and responses to his wife are sinful. She needs help to correct the problem. The negative attitude from her husband usually only causes additional conflicts, thus intensifying rather than correcting the problem.

Secondly, he should apologize to his wife for his negative response, according to Matthew 18:15, realizing also the truthfulness of Ephesians 5:23 which says, "For the husband is the head of the wife . . . ." He ought to ask her forgiveness for not having helped her correct her problem, as a proper leader should do.

Thirdly, the husband should seek God's proper response. A good response requires him to perhaps take his wife in his arms; tell her that he loves her; ask her how her day has gone; talk about things which may need discussing; then softly ask his wife if there is any reason why the house hasn't been cleaned. He might then offer to help her clean it.

Now obviously, since the husband might never have responded to his wife in this manner, and since he has developed the habit of a different response, a sinful one, he will probably "feel like" (think) he is a hypocrite. Satan usually sees to that. But as he continues to defy Satan, responding to his wife Scripturally, within several weeks the new Godly response will replace the old ungodly one as natural behavior. Jay Adams says that from three to four weeks are usually required for an action change to become comfortable and from six to eight weeks for the new behavior to actually replace the old and become second nature. Ultimately, the husband's new response will be just as natural as the old sinful one had once been. The immediate results will be a decrease in his anxiety, joy in his heart, and peace at home. God can now work through him to begin to alter his wife's sinful housekeeping habits.

Conclusion

Secular psychiatry confesses that man needs change in the areas of attitude and actions, and as discussed earlier suggests that change in his actions may be effected through changing man's attitude. Some liberal psychiatry (there's a lot of it around today) goes even farther in its teachings. Armed with a denial of the existence of God, thus a denial of the authority of His Word, this liberal teaching declares, "If it feels good, do it," or, "If it's right for you, it's right," etc. If we want to do a certain thing, we are told, we should do it. For to desire something and not do it isn't healthy and is hypocritical. Seeing the need for man's attitudes and actions to be one, we are urged to move our actions to match our errant attitude. In other words, we are told that a married man who wants to date other women isn't wrong if he does it. In order to reduce the possibility of mental and emotional pressure and in order not to be a hypocrite, the man should alter his actions (date other women) to match his attitudes (lusts), this brand of psychiatry teaches.

As mentioned earlier, God also wants our actions to match our attitudes. He, however, promises to move our attitude, making it proper, to correspond to proper Biblical behavior. God challenges the married man who desires to date other women to become obedient to the Scriptures in relation to his wife and to adultery. Through the man's obedience, God promises the man a new attitude, a new desire to remain faithful to Him and to his wife, while at the same time reducing his lust for other women.

The above illustrations might be applied to any situation known to man. Because we are creatures of habit and because God can change us, He will change us when we want it enough to respond His way. Thus a Christian has no excuse for retaining a sinful set of desires (attitudes) or for continuing to exercise his bad actions, reactions, or responses.

Man's basic problem, of course, is believing that he shouldn't be forced to do something he doesn't want to do. Our "desires" weigh heavier in us than our "desire to obey God." What we want to do is more important to us than what God wants us to do. The result is that we continue to wait for our "wanter" to change, that obedience might require no effort. God promises to change our "wanter" only through our obedience to Him. Man finds himself, therefore, at an impasse with God. When change occurs and man's lot improves, it will happen because man has adjusted to God, not the other way around.

VI APPLICATION

1 List some things you do by habit.

2 What are some "bad" things which you have, through the years, fallen into the habit of doing?

3 What are some "bad" responses and reactions toward your marriage partner which are done by habit?

4 Can you think of some Bible passages which tell you how you should respond and react to your marriage partner?

5 Examine yourself! Now that you have located the appropriate passages, do you still "desire" to respond and react wrongly? Can you change your desires? Who can?

6 Do you "really" believe that through your obedience to the Scriptures, God will change your desires and convert your bad habits into good ones?

7 Now, identify the one "bad" habit which you would most like to lose. Find God's scriptural answer to the habit, that is, what God commands you to do, rather than doing the bad thing. Will you determine to obey God when the impulse strikes you to do the "bad" thing?

8 Finally keep a record of how long it takes you to begin losing your desire for the "bad" thing; how long it takes you to completely or almost completely lose it.

9 Now, commit yourself to putting off every bad habit and putting on God's response.

VII

CATHETERIZATION, THE CLEANSING WORK OF THE WORD

If we are to live victorious Christian lives (and victorious married lives), we must experience power in our lives, power to say "no" to God's prohibitions and power to say "yes" to His imperatives. Power of that magnitude is not inherent in the natural, that is, the unsaved man. It must come to him from some outside source. That outside source, of course, is God working through the Bible as His indwelling Spirit applies His Word through our minds to our "hearts." A growing Christian will discover a continuing increase, not in the availability of divine power, for that remains constant, but in his desire to appropriate that power into his life.

God's child must observe certain laws of spiritual growth in order to grow into the likeness of the Lord Jesus Christ. A good prayer life must be developed. He ought to witness. Christian fellowship is necessary. I believe, however, that the key to prayer, witnessing, and proper fellowship lies in a saturational study of the Word of God, the Bible. "The Word of God is quick, and powerful, and sharper than any two-edged sword. . . ." (Hebrews 4:12) What does Hebrews 4:12 really teach us about God's Word?

Hebrews 4:12

First, the Bible reveals itself as a quick, that is, a living book. It is a book of life designed to teach people how to live meaningful, purposeful, and hopeful lives. The Bible will stir your soul. It clearly leads men to Jesus Christ. Then, when they come to him, it indisputably relates how they might walk with Him. The Bible remains the instrument through which God's Holy Spirit changes our lives.

The Bible has power. A novel might capture our interest for a while and might even bring tears to our eyes, but a novel has no power. It may tell us of a better way to live but it cannot furnish the life-changing energy by which we can do it. But God's Word can provide that energy. God's blessings are upon His Word. It will not return to Him void.

Finally, the Word of God is sharp. It cuts deeply into our souls. If we saturate our minds and hearts with it, it will convict us of our sins and shame those sins out of our lives. Oh that God's people would only believe Him when He tells them about the power and the purpose of His Word.

God provides no substitute, either in the family or individually, for a saturational study of His Word. Through committed study, God prepares us to be what He wants us to be and to do what He wants us to do, both individually and as a family. The following pages should explain what I mean.

Catheterization of the Word

"Now ye are clean through the word which I have spoken unto you." (John 15:3) WHAT A STATEMENT! Almost as exciting, however, as the statement itself is the original meaning of the word "clean." The Greek word is transliterated "katharoi," a form of the noun "katharos." The medical term *catheterize* originates from this Greek word. What does all of this detail mean? Simply this! As we study the Word of God it catheterizes our minds. That is, it drains away the bits and pieces of impurities, lust, anger, pride, and various other things which have collected there since last we pored over it.

Notice that the Word, specifically the words of Jesus but including everything recorded in the Bible, purifies. Prayer, witnessing, fellowship, good works all have important and specific parts in Christian growth, but they aren't intended to cleanse us. Only a study of God's Word is ordained to cleanse, that is, to catheterize our minds and spirits. That being the case then, we ought to spend time in the word every day in order to stay clean before our Lord.

"Study to shew thyself approved unto God, a workman that needeth not to be ashamed, rightly dividing the word of truth," God commands through

Paul in 2 Timothy 2:15. How do you study the Word of God? I believe a study of the Word consists of at least five steps.

How to Study the Word of God

1. Read the section of Scripture all the way through, prohibiting your mind from straying.

As you begin this five-step process of studying the Word of God, you will want to choose a book of the Bible. Let's say you have decided to study through the Gospel of John. The first day you might want to study chapter one. Get alone, away from the telephone, family, etc. You say, "I can't. My family is always present." My answer is "Yes, you can." It may mean you must struggle out of bed an hour or so earlier than usual, but you can do it. Check your priorities. If you really want to study the Bible, God will help you find the time.

Having decided to study the first chapter of John, and being alone, pray that God will open your mind and heart to His truths. Then read the chapter.

Guess what usually happens? Having read part of the chapter, perhaps to the well-known verse fourteen, you "wake up" and realize that you don't remember anything you've read from verse five. Your mind strayed. What do you do? Keep reading? I suspect that many Christians do. Do you go back to verse five and start again? A few Christians might. Neither of these, however, is what you should do. GO BACK TO VERSE ONE and begin again.

Finally, after you have returned to verse one several times, perhaps five to ten times (depending upon your concentration), you'll probably become disgusted with yourself. That's good, because now, by a sheer act of your will, you will force your mind to remain on what you're reading until you have read the entire chapter. Are you aware of what you have done? You have, by an act of your will, allowed the Holy Spirit to remove your mind from under Satan's control and place it under the control of God. Now you're ready for step two.

2. Read the chapter again verse by verse, sentence by sentence, or thought by thought.

Read the chapter again stopping where the thought stops. "Where does the thought stop?" you might ask. Usually you can determine where the thought changes without much difficulty. If, however, there is some question in your mind about it, just stop where there is a period. There may be several periods within one verse. There may be several verses between periods. Normally, complete thoughts fall between periods.

Let's for a moment assume that you have read John, chapter one (step one). Now read verse one again. The period is at the end of the verse so stop there. This brings you to step three.

3. Ask the question, "What is God saying in this verse?"

The third step consists of asking yourself, "What is God saying here?" Be prepared to think.

A current philosophy can be found floating around some evangelical-fundamental circles which suggests that a person who applies his mind to studying the Word of God is somehow unspiritual. I cannot begin to imagine how such a view ever wiggled its way into Bible-believing institutions. The Word of God certainly wasn't the source of it. We are commanded to study the Word (2 Timothy 2:15). I propose that one cannot study without concentrating, thus he must think about what he is reading. A good part of the book of Proverbs reinforces this truth. Studying God's Word must never stop at the level of intellect, but study does necessitate its use.

To answer the question "What is God saying?" you will probably be forced to think and to "wrestle" with the Scriptures. The Bible reflects a touch of the infinite mind of God against the finite brain of man. Without the enlightening work of the Holy Spirit as He illumines our minds to the meaning of God's Word, we cannot understand it. With His Spirit, the task often looms difficult. (Peter said Paul's writings were "hard to be understood," 2 Peter 3:16.) Wrestle with the verse, think about it, concentrate. After you have done this for awhile, God will probably open your mind to a truth in the verse, a truth which might have gone unnoticed before.

Now, let's return to John 1:1: *"In the beginning was the Word, and the Word was with God, and the Word was God."* What is God saying here? First, we will need to identify the meaning of "Word." From the Spirit-controlled reading of the chapter (step one) we remember that the Word became flesh (verse 14). The Word then is Christ. But what does *"In the beginning"* mean? Notice the preposition "in." God did not say "at the beginning," or "from the beginning," or "after the beginning." He said "in the beginning." In the beginning of all things which were created (1:3-4) Jesus already "was." That means He already existed. He was *"in the beginning,"* that is to say, eternal. He had no beginning.

The second phrase reads, *"and the Word was with God. . . ."* Jesus was with God. Notice the two Persons, the Word and God. "God" must be referring to God the Father. From eternity then, the Word, Jesus, was with God the Father. Think through all the ramifications of being "with" someone. Jesus had been with the Father from eternity past. They loved and knew one another perfectly. Their minds and hearts were in perfect unison. Now think through the horrors of the cross. For the first time in all eternity God removed Himself from fellowship with Jesus because He, Jesus, became black with my sin and yours. On the cross, Jesus was with God no longer. Think about that.

Finally, *"and the Word was God."* Jesus was God. He was not an angel or a created being. He was God, and every bit as much God as you are human. Think about that for a while. That One Who was placed in the body of a sinful woman, born into this world through the natural birth process, was eternal God, the Son. That One Who subjected Himself to the hatred of those whom He had created and He Who accepted our sin guilt, our evil, was none other than God. Don't be in a hurry to leave the verse. Mull over it, meditate upon it, think about what God is saying. When you believe you understand, go on to step four.

4. Ask the question, "How does this verse affect me today?"

It will not be difficult to determine how John 1:1 answers that question! When I consider that that One who left the love and peace of His Father and willingly came into the cesspool of this world to be contaminated with my filth, it ought to break my heart. The verse really denotes God's great love and concern for my wayward soul. Long before I was ever born, the Eternal Word Who was with God and Who was God had planned a journey; the journey would lead ultimately to the cross and provide the way for you and me, sinners, to be made acceptable to God. How does the verse affect me? It affects me far more than a home, or a good job, or riches. Those things are temporal and will pass away. But that given to me by the *Word* of verse one shall never pass away. The Eternal Word, Who was with God and Who was God, has heaped on top of the joy and peace of this life, the certainty that I will be with Him eternally. Now for the final step.

5. Obey the Word of God.

The final step in studying the Word of God is to obey it. If the verse contains a command (verse one obviously does not) the obedience is a simple thing. Just do what the verse commands you to do. However, if the verse is not a command, as illustrated by John 1:1, then obedience should flow from the answer to the question in step four. For example, when I realize how John 1:1 affects me, then I ought to submit to that effect upon me. The verse shows me God's love; His concern; the permanency of His relationship with me. I ought to allow God's Spirit to seal these truths to my heart and mind and I should live my life in full knowledge and appreciation of them. That means that I will strive to maintain my relationship with Jesus as I return His love and concern through obedience.

"And why call ye me, Lord, Lord, and do not the things which I say?" asks the Lord in Luke 6:46. ". . . If a man love me, he will keep my words . . . ." (John 14:23). Obedience then becomes the purpose for Bible study. Apparently one cannot have studied the Bible until he has obeyed it.

Application

Through this kind of a saturational study of the Bible, God applies His spiritual truths to man's spiritual weaknesses. When our minds are invested in a concentrated study of His Word, as mentioned, God will emit from the Scriptures truths designed to minister to our failings. It is medicine applied to a sore. The Word of God heals our spiritual infirmities. That being the case, it becomes our greatest defensive weapon against the attacks of Satan. I had not been a Christian very long when I discovered a great truth. As my mind began to dwell upon past sins and godless relationships, I would actually experience a weakening of my moral resistance.

But as I committed my mind to a saturational study of the Scriptures, I would experience a strengthening spirit. The implanted Word would erase and overcome the sinful thoughts by draining them from my mind. I believe I could have charted the change on a graph. Away from the Word of God, I encountered bad thoughts! When I studied the Word of God saturationally, the thoughts decreased correspondingly. Oh, what a weapon for overcoming the attacks of Satan we often leave untouched!

I wonder how many Christians ever really study the Bible? I doubt seriously that many ever get to step two. Most of them probably do not even successfully complete step one. I question whether any Christian can be "cleansed" until God is allowed to catheterize his mind through this or a similar kind of saturational study of His Word.

Frankly, I confess that I must continue to study this way each day in order to accomplish that to which God has called me. I have already discovered, the hard way, that if I fail to study the Word of God for three successive days, the "bits and pieces" of sin collect in my mind from day to day, causing me to lose control of my thought life. When someone pulls his automobile out in front of mine, for example, I might lose control of my temper. When someone criticizes me, I might experience animosity toward him.

God did not spend 1600 years and all that effort to give us His Word for no reason. He wants us, and commands us, to spend time in the Bible so that He might clean out the dark recesses of our minds. Please, folks, determine now to spend time each day in His Word. Allow Him to drain the impure thoughts from your mind daily so that they might never accumulate and evolve into physical impurity.

Conclusion

Now, what does all of that have to do with marital problems? If the Word can catheterize thoughts of sin, desires, lusts, etc., from our minds, why cannot it also drain away animosities, bitternesses, or hatreds toward our marriage partners? The answer, as you might have guessed, is, "It can." Many of us, however, had rather nurse our anger than lose it. Our pride begs us to retain it for a possible future weapon.

Foy, my wife, will not mind me sharing one of her characteristics with you (I hope). She is very forgetful. (I could have said "absent-minded" but "forgetful" sounds better.) I have seen her put boiled eggs, hot off the stove, into the dishwasher. You would never believe some of the places she has deposited her rings and car keys. Historically, we invest a notable part of our week in searching for them. Once, the entire family looked for her rings for several hours in, of all places, the front yard. She had taken them off to work in the flower bed and had laid them down in the grass. Just today I watched her empty a large box of Sweet 'n Low packets into a cannister, walk to the food pantry, remove a bag of sugar and proceed to pour the sugar into the Sweet 'n Low box. All these acts are humorous, even to me, now, but before I was a Christian, they disgusted me. I want everything "in its place." I dislike being forced to look for a tool, or a newspaper, or car keys. I place everything in a certain spot and expect to find it there when I need it. Frankly, looking for the eggs in the dishwasher never occurs to me.

When God put our marriage back together, I quickly discovered that Foy still had the fantastic ability to misplace things. I also discovered that I still possessed the capacity to become disgusted with her for doing it. I likewise soon found that the Word of God could catheterize the disgust from my mind as perfectly as it could drain away impure thoughts. Because of the changing power of God's Word, that which once was disgusting has become humorous. Only God can do that and He does it as we make a concerted effort to saturate our minds with His Word. And life certainly is more enjoyable when laughter replaces disgust.

VII *APPLICATION*

1 In the depth of your soul, do you really believe that all the Bible is written by God through human writers? Is the Bible actually your final authority? What does final authority mean to you?

2 How much time do you spend in "reading" the Bible each day? In studying it?

3 What is the difference between reading and studying?

4 In light of the information in this chapter, why do you suppose Satan seems to be attempting to discredit the inerrancy of the Scriptures?

5 List your "secret" sins (thoughts, lusts, etc.) on a piece of paper. (You will probably want to keep this list in a "private" or "secret" place.) Now, ask yourself, "Do I really want to be freed from them or do I enjoy them and want to keep them?"

6 If you want to lose these sins, begin to study through the Scriptures. Everytime a verse ministers to you in one of these areas, write down the reference beside the specific sin. At the end of a month go over these Scriptures again and see how many times God has spoken to that specific area.

7 Study through Psalms 119, giving special attention to verses which emphasize the cleansing work of the Word, like 119:9.

VIII

EVIL PLUS GOD EQUALS GOOD

"There is no way," loudly declares the lady. "There is no way any good can come out of this." Thus once again, however unintentionally, one of God's creatures denies His clear, Scriptural teachings. For a Christian facing difficulty, the "problem" is never "the problem." The problem is the Christian's response to the problem. The Bible teaches that every complexity which enters the Christian's life, regardless of how evil or life-consuming it might be, offers God the opportunity of converting the problem into good upon the Christian's scriptural response to it. In other words, everything "bad" that happens to you and me will be converted into "good" if we respond to it God's way.

All Things? For Good?

Romans 8:28 probably teaches that truth more clearly than any other Scripture. "*And we know that all things work together for good to them that love God, to them who are the called according to his purpose."* What a "loaded" verse! What a message! It isn't by accident either that verse 28 follows a section of Scripture which carefully establishes several related truths: the conflict between the Spirit and the flesh; sufferings encountered because we have been born into a world groaning with its imperfections; and the work of the Holy Spirit in our infirmities. Also verse 28 precedes, not accidentally, Scripture which confirms a Christian's position in relation to God. Notice carefully the words of the verse.

"And we know." Christian, child of God, you ought to know that the Word of God is true and that God our Father wants (as any good father would) to help us grow, not tear us down. Paul says it is something to be known. It should not even be questioned.

"All things." The verse teaches that nothing enters into life accidentally. Both those things which are "good" and those things which are "bad" are ushered into my life, neither of them by accident. Both are designed, not to lessen my effectiveness in the Christian walk, but to enhance it. Even though Satan may be found at the source of my troubles (the bad things) and has thrust them into my life to perhaps spiritually cripple or destroy me, God has guaranteed to strengthen me through even these bad things. All things then, whether good or bad, will ultimately lodge on the positive side of the ledger of my life as I respond to them Scripturally.

"Work." God promises that these things, all

things, are at work. They are not stagnant, meaning-
less events. They are designed to work change in
my life, to take me from "where I am" to "where
God wants me to be."

"Together for good." All the things that happen
to me are lumped together. Oh, how we need to
"get hold" of that truth. God utilizes all things for
the same purpose in my life. I tend to view the good
and bad as opposites. Not God! He sees the result of
all of them, therefore He labels all of them "good,"
because He plans to accomplish good through all of
them. Understand, please, that I'm not accusing
God of viewing sin as "good." But He does seem to
view even sin as an instrument through which good
can be accomplished.

"Them that love God." God directs His covenant
promises toward them that love Him and are called
by Him. God promises His children that no evil can
enter into their lives which He will not convert into
good, contingent, of course, upon their Scriptural
response. Do you see the impact of this truth?
Christians need fear neither circumstance, problem, nor person. Christians need never be consumed by worry or anxiety. Christians need never
"kick against the pricks" (Acts 9:5) but instead
should be able to accept whatever comes their way,
knowing that the final state of the thing will be
good. Therein lies real freedom, knowing that the
evil which contaminates my life will be converted
into good as I respond to it God's way. The effect of
trouble upon our lives, then, cannot be laid to our
Lord's account. If the evil produces no good in us,

our unscriptural response to it supplies the reason why.

Joseph—No Bitterness—No Hatred!

Perhaps one of the clearest examples of this truth issues from the life of Joseph. You certainly remember the story, recorded in Genesis 37-50. Joseph, one of the twelve sons of Jacob (who was a "father' of Israel), was hated and rejected by his brothers. Out in the field one day they cast Joseph down into a pit, where he might have died. Judah, though, persuaded the brothers to sell Joseph to a group of Midianite merchantmen who were traveling in a caravan to Egypt. The brothers later convinced their father Jacob that Joseph was dead.

What could be worse than slavery, especially to a young, free Hebrew, a member of the chosen family of God? Could death be worse? Not for God's child, for death only furnishes a passageway into His blessed presence. Joseph suffered a worse tragedy. But when you read carefully through the pages of his story, something becomes glaringly obvious. Joseph harbored no bitterness, not even when falsely accused of attempted rape by Potiphar's wife and thrown into prison. When the butler failed to fulfill Joseph's request concerning his release from prison, he continued to be void of hatred. For years he was persecuted and he suffered for things which he did not do, yet without bitterness. Finally, because of God's influence in his life, Joseph was promoted to the second position of power and responsibility in all the land. Only Pharaoh himself ruled over him. The stage was now set for God to accomplish the purpose for which Joseph had suffered.

When Joseph finally identified himself to his brothers, ". . . his brethren could not answer him, for they were troubled (terrified) at his presence." Had there been vengeance in Joseph, he now found himself with the perfect opportunity to exercise it. But he didn't. The forgiveness for his own sins must have mellowed and tempered his heart. Joseph's great love controlled his words as he identified himself to his brothers:

"Come near to me, I pray you. And they came near. And he said, I am Joseph your brother, whom ye sold into Egypt. Now therefore be not grieved, nor angry with yourselves, that ye sold me hither: for GOD DID SEND ME before you to preserve life . . . And God sent me before you to preserve you a posterity in the earth, and to save your lives by a great deliverance. So now it was not you that sent me hither, BUT GOD . . . ." (Genesis 45:4-8, emphasis mine)

What thought-provoking yet comforting words! A dynamic truth about God emerges from these verses. Even though Satan working through the impiety of the brothers' hearts could be found at the source of their sinful deed, God allowed the evil sale of Joseph to occur in order to accomplish His will. What a testimony to the grace of God! What a picture of His power! What a tribute to His sovereign majesty! What a promise from our covenant-keeping God! What an illustration of Him working with His children as He battles the evil one on our behalf! You see, child of God, nothing, absolutely nothing, can penetrate your life which, upon your scriptural response to it, cannot be turned into good. Joseph must have understood God perfectly, because he was able to say, "You sold me but God sent me." When Joseph accepted, without question, what had happened to him, God was able to fulfill His purpose in Joseph's life. Oh the peace that comes from knowing I'm in God's hand! Oh the freedom of not having to hate those who hurt me! Oh the joy of knowing that even my pain will be used by God to form and fashion my life and make me more like Jesus!

Friend, brother, sister, what has Satan brought into your life? Have you lost a loved one through divorce? Allow God to erase all bitterness and hatred so that He can work in your life and perhaps in the spouse's life or even in a third party's life. Has Satan delivered to you a painful "thorn in the flesh," a problem of some sort perhaps with your health or finances? Then like the Apostle Paul in 2 Corinthians 12:9b, recognizes that the thorn can be used for your good.

Paul—A Man Who Gloried in Pain

"Most gladly therefore will I rather glory in my infirmities, that the power of Christ may rest upon me." Paul had asked the Lord three times to ease the pain but God answered Paul's prayer a different way. God reminded him, "My grace is sufficient for thee: for my strength is made perfect in weakness." The sovereign God needed a "suffering" servant, not a "comfortable" one. And besides, Paul, like a lot of us, could not stand prosperity. He tended to become proud. So God simply backed away from Paul and allowed Satan to have a go at him. When the Apostle accepted the pain rather than bitterly condemning it, God then accomplished good through it.

No problem exists, no temptation or trial, no pain so severe that God cannot convert it into strength for us. God has promised to do it, Christian. God requires only that we respond and react to it according to His Word.

Job—A Suffering Servant

I am convinced that all Christians should carefully study through the book of Job at least once a year. Job had everything: money, family, wealth, health, fame, prestige. You name it—he had it. He loved God, and God wanted to use him to present to the culture of his day and, through the recorded pages of Holy Writ, to our world, a picture of how He, God, works through Satan's persecutions. God had every right to allow Satan to persecute Job. God created Job and blessed him with all that he owned. What happened to Job was God's business, His affair. If He wanted to allow Job to lose everything, who could call Him unjust?

You and I look at ourselves through our own selfish eyes. Often we fail or deliberately refuse to acknowledge God's ownership of us. However, we are His with which to do as He deems fit. He cannot be accused of being unjust regardless of what He allows to happen to us.

Paul corrected a similar Roman attitude, explaining that God had authority to use any vessel He chose to use. God had chosen to use Jacob. Paul, anticipating that some men would accuse God of having been unjust by not allowing Esau equal opportunity, replied,

> What shall we say then? Is there unrighteousness with God? God forbid (May it never be). For he saith to Moses, I will have mercy on whom I will have mercy, and I will have compassion on whom I will have compassion. So then it is not of him that willeth, nor of him that runneth, but of God that sheweth mercy. For the scripture saith unto Pharaoh, Even for this same purpose have I raised thee up, that I MIGHT SHEW MY POWER IN THEE, and that my name might be declared throughout all the earth. Therefore hath he mercy on whom he will have mercy, and whom he will he hardeneth. (Romans 9:14-18, emphasis mine)

Paul anticipated that the Roman church and some of us today might "kick" against these truths, i.e., that God has sovereign rights over all flesh; therefore he wrote verses 19-23.

> Thou wilt say then unto me, Why doth he yet find fault? For who hath resisted His will? Nay but, O man, who art thou that repliest against God? Shall the thing formed say to him that formed it, Why hast thou made me thus? Hath not the potter power over the clay, of the same lump to make one vessel unto honour, and another unto dishonour? What if God, willing to shew His wrath, and to make His power known, endured with much longsuffering the vessels of

> wrath fitted to destruction: And that he might make
> known the riches of his glory on the vessels of mercy,
> which he had afore prepared unto glory.

Paul quickly heads off the resistance to these truths which he knows will come. He anticipated that his readers would deny God the right to use those in whom He chose to illustrate His power, like Pharoah and Esau (whom He did not choose to bless). Paul's prepared answer is instant and precise. "Nay but, O man, who art thou that repliest against God?" The thing formed, man, has no right to question the One Who did the forming, God. Man, when he hurts, often wants to replace God's concept of justice with his own. God establishes the standard for justice, not man. As soon as God does a thing, that makes it right. Man ought never to question it. God has every right to use us in any way He deems necessary in order to accomplish His will. While being used may discomfort us for the present, we will rejoice in eternity that He so chose to bless us. Should not we then rejoice now?

The situation finally boils down to this: God allows things to happen to me for a purpose; and He has a right to do with and through me what He wills to do. I must respond to my trials as God in His Word commands me to respond. That is my calling. When I respond scripturally, then God will convert the problem into strength and He will, through the problem, change my life more into the likeness of Jesus Christ. As a matter of fact, suffering, rather than being adverse to the Christian life, provides a certain, desired, necessary part of it.

Second Timothy 3:12 declares, "Yea, and all that will live godly in Christ Jesus shall suffer persecution." Paul says in Philippians 1:29, "For unto you it is given in the behalf of Christ, not only to believe on him, but also to suffer for his sake." Paul continues in 3:10, "That I may know him, and the power of his resurrection, and the fellowship of his sufferings, being made comformable to his death."

In order, then, to procure from the Christian life all that our Lord would have us gain, we must suffer. And why not? Jesus suffered. Why would suffering not be a part of the Christian life? Certainly, though, no rational person pursues it. Pain isn't fun in any form, but it sometimes seems to be necessary in order for the spirit to be victorious over the flesh. Through the pain of a buffeted body, I find myself more spiritually inclined. Simply put, when I hurt, I pray, and study the Word, and attempt to walk as close to the Source of comfort as I possibly can, that being Jesus.

The early church knew little but suffering. Until Christianity was declared a legal religion by Constantine in A.D. 315, Christians suffered all kinds of persecution, even death. Through the ages, in various areas of the world, Christians have suffered for their faith, the most recent one being Uganda where, under the demon-controlled Idi Amin, thousands of Christians were martyred. Only by the grace of God have Christians not suffered in this land. But times are changing. American Christians, while we should never pursue persecution, may nevertheless face it. May God grant us the grace to endure it as have others throughout the centuries.

Therefore, regardless of why the problem has come into your life; whether it be designed by Satan to wreck you, or by God to chasten you; or whether it comes because of your faith in Jesus, or because of your own weaknesses, comfort issues from knowing that God can convert it into your good! The key, once again, is your reaction. Have you accepted the problem with thanksgiving, or are you bitterly kicking against it?

Conclusion

"There is no way any good can come out of this," the lady cries. Oh, yes! God can accomplish good, even through a wayward husband's escapades, when the wife responds to the problem scripturally. Listen Christian, because God has promised freedom to everyone (it is part of His law), He must allow each person to exercise that freedom: freedom to come to Him; freedom to sin; freedom to hurt those who love Him. For God to restrict that promised freedom, He would, like Lucifer, become a law-breaker Himself. But God cannot sin. Therefore, He must allow every person freedom. Now once again, Christian, heed the beautiful part: In essence God says to you, "Child, I must give every person freedom and I know you may be hurt because of it. But understand how I work, accept it, and react to it like I've written, and I will turn your hurt into good. Please trust Me."

Friends, the issue boils down to trust. Do we

trust God! He promises to turn all the evil, pain, and hurt which enters our lives into good. The only question is, "Do you believe Him?" Remember, for a Christian, the problem is never the problem. For us, the problem is our response to the problem.

VIII *APPLICATION*

1   Read the introduction to the chapter again. Do you believe the last sentence of the introduction?

2   How do you personally distinguish between the "good" and "bad" which happens to you?

3   List all the "bad" things which have happened, or are even now happening to you. Can you see any "good" in them?

4   What is your "heart" attitude about these "bad" things? Do you possess any bitterness because of them? If you do, toward whom are you directing that bitterness?

5   Thinking back, consider the "bad" things which have occured to you in the past. How many of these things have you responded to with a grateful, trusting heart? Has any good, so far as you can determine, come from them?

6   With the list of "bad" things which have burdened you, and with a concordance (if you do not know the Scripture), look up the Scripture concerning God's response to the problem.

7   Thank God for the opportunity to see Him convert "bad" into good. Stop deliberately thinking about the problem. When you cannot seem to free your mind from thinking about the problem, prayerfully saturate your mind with the Word according to the principles discussed in Chapter 7.

IX

WHAT ABOUT YOUR CHILDREN?

A Strange Thing

An extraordinary attitude has emerged in many parents with whom I have counseled through the past few years. Amidst the agony of marital problems, few have expressed genuine concern for their children. Could it be that in the face of problems and adversity, we parents become so self-centered and fearful that we forget the children? The question seems to be a harsh one, but frankly, very few suffering parents, burdened by marital difficulty, appear to be as concerned about the children as they are about themselves. If selfishness and fear are in fact the causes of this phenomenon, then no wonder at the rebellion which often surfaces in young people today!

Several erroneous concepts emanate from the contemporary American culture. First, children are unscathed by husband-wife problems; second, because they very often say little or nothing they therefore are not really conscious of family problems; and third, since they are young, they can rebound quickly from emotional distress. Not one of these things, of course, is true.

Children Are Hurt by Divorce

First, children are not unscathed by husband-wife problems. They are touched very deeply, not only by separation and divorce, but by every snide, unloving, critical remark made by one parent to the other. A child does not need to understand that one parent has committed immorality, for example, in order to be damaged by the ensuing hate and bitterness flowing from the hurt parent. Likewise, a child is hardly ever so young as to be totally oblivious to impatience, coldness, and hatred. Their little minds register fear automatically when they are in the presence of fighting parents. As a matter of fact, children need not be in the presence of fighting parents in order for them to know that something is wrong. (I am not certain why God has so designed children, only that He has done so. Perhaps it is for self-preservation.) Subjectively, a child often knows to shy away from an angry parent even before the parent actually erupts into violence. What conflict rages inside a child's heart when he sees and hears his parents hurl condemnation at one another! On the one hand, the youngster's love and respect for his parents draws him to them. On the other hand, because of the parents' hostility toward one another, in fear he recedes from them. What a horrible conflict! Yet equally as horrible is the fact that the child did not cause the problem and can do nothing to temper nor prevent it. He or she only suffers as the victim of it.

Because of a child's intellectual immaturity and emotional instability, few of them are capable of coping with parental and/or marital difficulty. The child often seems to ignore the fights. But because the child fails to respond outwardly to the fights does not prove that he is unconscious of them. As a matter of fact, it might indicate that the hurt, fear, and uncertainty are so great that he escapes from the reality of the pain by refusing to acknowledge the existence of the problem. Parents ought not to be lulled into thinking that simply because the child no longer reacts to family problems that he is not hurting. He is! Parents should face that fact and they should make any necessary sacrifice to insure that children are not subjected to hatred of any kind.

Thirdly, some parents of young children seem to believe their children will easily rebound from any traumatic emotional distress. Consequently the parents might subconsciously conclude, "Let's 'unload' on one another. The children will get over it!" Nothing could be farther from the truth. The children will never "get over it," if by getting over it one means that it will not affect their lives. Everything parents do forms and fashions the lives of their children. When the child becomes an adult and a Christian, he may be able to overcome the affects of the trauma, but the memory of it will always be with him. It may, in fact, influence the rearing of his own children.

Children Imitate Parents

God seems to have built into the nature of a child the propensity to emulate his parents. A boy will tend to imitate his father and a girl often reflects the character qualities of the mother. Therefore God encourages parents, through scriptural principles, to imitate Jesus by living Godly lives. Thus when the child imitates the parents, he will have formed and fashioned within him the character qualities of Jesus. But what if the parents follow, not the Lord Jesus, but the world? What if they live ungodly lives? The child, "programmed" by God, continues to copy the parents' behavior. He then becomes an ungodly reflection of the parents. Someone has said, "We reproduce ourselves in our children." The television commercial which urges parents to stop smoking asks a profound question: "Like father, like son?" Perhaps that explains the true meaning of Exodus 34:7 and Numbers 14:18. Both verses declare that God will visit the iniquity of the fathers upon the children and upon the children's children to the third and fourth generation.

God tells us to train up our children in the way they should go and when they are old they will not depart from it (Proverbs 22:6). There have been many renderings of Proverbs 22:6, but it tells me that lifestyles are basically established in the beginning of our lives. Those character qualities gained in our formative years become so ingrained that only "divine surgery," can eliminate the bad ones.

As parents, may God break our hearts over our responsibility to impute Godly behavior patterns to our children. May Christian parents particularly understand that the very same things which our children see in us will be observed again, only the next time around the parents will see them in the children!

Can Divorce Be Best For the Child?

One of the comments which flows across my desk frequently goes something like this: "I know divorce isn't the best way but I really believe the children will be better off, what with all the fighting and fussing they see and hear!" By the time that statement is completed, I am usually "cocked and ready!" What a "cop-out," as the younger generation would say! Now, I am conscious (and was once a part) of the concept in American society which has sold us on the idea that parents have a right to happiness even if it means hurting the children, a view, incidentally, which is completely unauthorized by Scripture. But when people yield to that concept and get their divorce, guilt usually follows. That kind of guilt often produces overcompensation toward the children. Overcompensation allows the children freedom to enter certain areas which are restricted by God. Capitulation here often becomes a type of "buy-off" and it has produced the unscriptural ideas of "child rights" (having nothing to do with ungodly child abuse, which Scripture clearly forbids) and the International Year of the Child.

"Let us live our lives as we want to live them, children," adults seem to be saying, "and we'll allow you the freedom to run your own lives." Thus parents damage their children even farther while soothing their own consciences. "How are the children damaged by that?" you might ask. Here's how! Children need boundaries around their lives. Subconsciously they realize that they cannot cope with the gigantic problems which face them! They are especially vulnerable to peer pressure, an instrument in the hand of Satan by which many young people plunge into sin. They are, if not consciously, then certainly to a degree subconsciously, aware that in their youth, they cannot know the final outcome of everything with which they experiment. Their brains have not matured to the point where they can reason through all of their problems. Therefore children need adults to supply boundaries around their lives, thereby establishing areas into which they cannot move. These "forbidden" areas, outlining that which is "allowable," form the basis for security in the young person's life. When he discovers clear boundaries, he experiences considerably less pressure from his peers. He simply states, "I cannot do that, I would be disciplined for it by my parents, I would lose some of my freedoms, etc." This delivers the young person from the stigma attached by saying, "I won't do that" to his friends. It wasn't him that said "no," it was his parents. Clearly defined forbidden and unforbidden areas therefore remove from the youth the responsibility for his refusal to participate in sinful activity. As the young person obeys his parents, the responsibility rests squarely where it should, upon the parents. When the parents establish the rules, and the children follow them, the children aren't forced to cope with the world's gigantic problems, at least, not all of them. The parents make those decisions for the young person, which frees the youth to enjoy the things he ought to enjoy. Finally, by establishing boundaries around their children's lives, parents assume the responsibility for having thought through the problems, hopefully with adult wisdom and experience. They have relieved their children of the impossible task of reasoning through difficult problems with an immature mind. All of this gives something to our children which they need desperately . . . security. Security brings a peace to the heart of a young person thereby relieving him of searching for it. (That search was discussed in chapter two.) It frees the mind and heart of young people from the slavery of overt sin and allows them to enjoy their youth.

An Increase In Unrest

"Is that why we seem to be witnessing more and more unrest in our young people?", you might ask. Are we forcing them to make adult decisions with a child's intellect and experience? I believe that is precisely what we see occurring in our culture today. Furthermore I believe the basic reasons for it are twofold. One has already been mentioned, i.e., that in order to soothe our consciences for our ineptitude as parents, we have "bought off" our children with almost "blanket" freedom. As discussed, this further complicates the matter because it deprives the child of desperately needed boundaries around his life, which produce security. But secondly (and this reason relates closely to the first), adults no longer seem to be interested in training their youth; they want instead to become one. Consequently our entire culture seems to be youth-oriented. The wisdom and experience of adulthood are depreciated and the mental inability and lack of experience of youth are fantacized. In the meantime, even some Christians, in a "last-ditch" effort to stay young, conceal their age, dye their gray hair, and dress like their teen-age children or grandchildren. To ask an adult's age in our culture breaches common etiquette, and gray hair has become such an abomination that millions of dollars are spent each year to hide it. What produces America's attitude toward age? Certainly not the Scriptures. God very carefully declared publicly many of His great servants' ages. Whereas our culture condemns age and hopelessly attempts to conceal it, God honors it when it's found in a Godly person. In the Proverbs He says, "The glory of young men is their strength: and the beauty of old men is the grey head" (20:29). Again, in 16:31, "The hoary (grey) head is a crown of glory, if it be found in the way of righteousness" (parenthesis mine). Leviticus 19:32 commands, "Thou shalt rise up before the hoary (grey) head, and honor the face of

the old man . . . ." Honor the face of the old man!
Why, our culture not only considers honoring the
face of the aged passe' but many old men and
women do all science and medicine permit in order
to obscure the age in their faces. Not only that, but
our culture labels it a distinct offense to refer to
someone as old, even though God does. As a matter
of fact, that's what He did in Leviticus 19:32.

Several years ago I was Dean of Students at a
small Bible College. One of our students was a
refugee from Idi Amin's Uganda. He, his wife, and
five children fled when they discovered that Amin
had placed them on his now-infamous death list.
Through a mission organization which was head-
quartered in a city near the Bible College where I
served, this precious family found its way into our
student body. As you might expect, because of his
experiences the man was invited to share his
testimony many times. One day he spoke to the
senior adults of a local, evangelical church whose
pastor was my close personal friend. In the dear
Ugandan brother's introductory statements he said
in his broken English, "Ladies and gentlemen, it is a
pleasure for me to be here with you old men and
women." In Uganda, ungodly under Amin as the
nation was, to refer to someone as "old" was a
compliment. It meant you recognized his wisdom,
experience, and authority. But it isn't a compliment
in America! The comment was such an offense that
the Bible College president deemed it necessary to
make an apology to the church. Can you imagine
Christians being offended by a Scriptural state-

ment? Yes, you can, because Satan has done a masterful job of bringing some of his concepts even into the sacred halls of Bible-believing churches, perhaps even yours. The very fact that you might have viewed the Ugandan's statement as either humorous or in bad taste proves that Satan has found a resting place for some of his doctrine in your heart. That's why it is so important that we stop succumbing to false concepts and begin to reinstate God's teachings even in our "small talk." Almost every day I hear people joking about age. "But wait now!" you might reply. "Isn't that just a little bit legalistic? After all as long as people are joking about it, it means they aren't taking age too seriously." Well, there are two answers to that. First, jokes are usually made about basic truths. The cartoon satirist who draws the humorous images on the editorial page of the newspaper proves that fact. Therefore the "jokes" may not be jokes at all. Secondly, age really is not a joking matter. It ought to be viewed as a serious and sobering process designed to draw from all of us a sober look at our life of service (or lack of it) to the Lord.

Who's Most Important?

Divorce also clearly announces to the children that one parent, at least, places more importance upon his own "happiness" than upon theirs. Furthermore no amount of "sugar-coating" can convince children any differently. The "sugar-coating" obviously convinces judges, lawyers, and most of

America's citizenry, but it will not persuade the child whose life has been torn by divorce. A youth has not become "sophisticated" or "civilized" enough to understand why his father and mother should love themselves more than they love him. I must now make a confession: neither have I. After all, the female dog is willing to suffer discomfort in order to protect her newly-born offspring, even to the point of death. Why should human parents be expected to do any less?

I Never Got Mad at Mother

Because of adult's improper attitudes and unscriptural actions toward our youth, many children have developed little respect for authority, parental or otherwise. With the lack of respect for authority comes the idea that the roles of young people are just as important as those of adults and that they deserve just as much respect and privilege. This concept leads to the notion that youth have the right to express anger or disgust toward their superiors. However, as related at the first of this section, an improper attitude in a child ultimately traces its way back to the parents. When the parents bring love and discipline into the children's lives, the children will for the most part reveal a distinct respect for that parent. I have already mentioned that parents should both discipline and love their children. These are broad terms. Discipline and love are demonstrated in the lives of young people through parental interest. Parents, where in your circles of interest do your children stand?

"What are circles of interest?" you might exclaim. To answer, I believe that each person possesses three circles of interest into which all his
activities fall, as illustrated below.

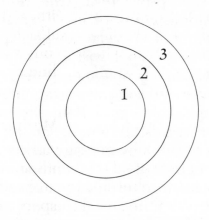

In the innermost circle of interest, number one, lie
those things which are nearest and dearest to your
heart. For a Christian, God should be at the very
center. The immediate family, other Christians, and
church activities should also be there. Before I
became a Christian, though, golf, party friends, and
parties, along with certain sins, were in the first
circle of my interests, along with myself. I occupied
God's place in dead center. What happens when
things in the innermost circle break down? You and
I do not spend time fussing and complaining about
the problem. They are so precious that we get the
things repaired pronto. Before salvation, when my
golf cart broke down, I loaded it on a pickup truck
and hauled it to a repair shop. It was of vital interest

to me. I did not fuss and fume about it. I spent whatever time and whatever effort was necessary to get it fixed, and I did not waste time complaining about it.

Prior to accepting Jesus, the things in the second or middle circle of my interest were my businesses, some of my relatives perhaps, the National Guard of which I was a member, football games, etc. When a problem arose in any of these areas, I experienced some aggravation but I would eventually make some kind of an effort to solve it. Enough interest existed to motivate me to tend to the problem but usually not right away.

The outer circle of interest housed my wife and children, our home, church and civic activities, etc. Now when these things broke down and needed my attention, they were pure aggravations because they were not very important to me. When my children broke down (had problems), I would often grow angry and with hardness in my voice say, "Don't bother me with that. Go see your mother about it. Can't you see I'm busy now?" (Usually "busy" meant trying to get to the golf course!) Can you imagine the effect of my attitude upon my precious little girl and boy? They became aware, even at their young ages, that they were not very important to me. Hurt turned to bitterness and rebellion with each passing year. You see, we spend the necessary time and effort to solve problems which lie at the center of our interest, but we do not usually want to be bothered with problems in the outer fringe. They are irritations.

I continue to be amazed at the enthusiasm with which the father, especially, invests great amounts of time into his business or golf game. With great patience he awaits progress, while at the same time, he denies his children both time and patience. Yet he wants his son to act like a thirty-year-old, mature man. Friends, whether we like it or not, it takes a great deal of time and patience to develop a young person into a responsible adult, perhaps even more than a business or golf game requires. Therefore, parents must be certain that their children abide in the inner circle of their interest, for time and patience will always be invested there.

Perhaps another reason many fathers, in particular, expect their sons to conduct themselves like mature adults (other than the fact that a child's problems are nuisances to the father when the child abides in the outer circle of his interests) is because we live in an "instant" world. Often parents, having grown accustomed to instant pleasure, comfort, service, and amusement, find themselves demanding instant perfection from their children. May I hasten to say, parents, you will not realize that expectation. Fathers, if you want your son to throw a ball like a man, you ought to spend time training him. If you want him to hunt with you, don't expect him to be suddenly capable of killing a flying quail. Many fathers expect their sons to accomplish adult actions, while at the same time they refuse to spend time training their sons to achieve these endeavors. Spend time teaching your son how to shoot a BB gun, fathers, before you expect him to be an expert marksman with a rifle.

Mothers, of course the same thing is true with you and your daughters. Time and effort are required in order to produce a young lady.

Therefore, my friends, with tears I caution you. In America there seem to be far more children in the outer circle of the parents' interest than in the inner circle. Please understand that the outer circle is Satan's breeding ground for childhood rebellion. Most likely your children will never grow into responsible men and women if they are reared in the third circle of your interests.

A Look Back—!

After I became a Christian and realized what I had done to my children, I began to think back to my childhood. My dad worked away from home and my mother, my sister Wanda, and I lived with my grandmother. Wanda and I were in the dead center of my mother's interest. When we had "breakdowns," problems, she tended to them immediately. What that did, although I certainly did not realize it at the time, was to build within me a deep love and respect for my mother. I never questioned her love for me, either inwardly or outwardly. Later, when I began living in deep sin, divorced and destitute, my mother, of course, was hurt. Through it all, however, I do not remember "raising my voice" toward her. I threatened to kill others who attempted to help me and who loved me just as much as she, but I responded with love and respect to her. I never even had a bad thought about her. Why this commitment and love for my mother when I loved no one else? Probably several reasons: I knew Mother loved me because she always ardently dropped whatever she was doing to tend to my needs. I never heard my mother "raise her voice" to me, or to anyone else. And she disciplined me in love. My friends, in my mother's actions, may I present to you part of the answer to our youth's problems today?! Couple all of my mother's love and wisdom with a strong commitment to Jesus and most parent-children problems can be solved. Satan faces a very difficult task when he tries to make an inroad into a home characterized by that kind of relationship.

Who's Controlling the Emotions

Placing the children in the second or outer circle of our interest produces another bad result. The children tend to control the emotional state of the family. As stated previously, when those things which are in the innermost circle of interest break down, we don't usually "fly off the handle" because they are so important to us. We tend to their needs. Usually, however, we grow irritated when things in the outer or third circle of our interest break down. They are not pre-eminent, therefore we will not invest the time and effort necessary to solve the problems. They just continue to be irritations, drawing out of us anger, disgust, dismay and other bad attitudes; thus they tend to control our emotions.

When children fall into the third circle of their parents' interest, as mentioned above, they set the emotional tone of the family. Of course those precious boys and girls do not fully realize it, nor do they do it intentionally, but they, rather than the parents, actually control the family's emotional condition.

Let's examine how it works. A boy, let's say, does not receive much attention from his father. The son is not capable of thinking through all of this, but subconsciously he realizes that his father appears to be more interested in work, golf, tennis, parties, reading the paper, watching television, or any number of other things than spending time with him. As the son grows older, the hurt of parental rejection begins to surface as resentment, bitterness, and rebellion. Two things frequently happen and they often occur simultaneously. Both thrust turmoil into the family. First, because the father continually considers other interests more important than his son (whether intentionally or not), when the boy breaks down (has a problem) the father may not want to be involved. He might tell his son not to bother him by sending him to his mother, or perhaps "put him off" by promising to handle the situation later. For whatever reason, the rejected son experiences hurt. Secondly, rebellion then begins to creep into the boy's heart. He eventually becomes unmanageable and hostile (perhaps not openly at first) toward his father. The hostility usually emerges when the father tells his son to perform a certain chore (like taking out the garbage or cutting the grass) and the son complains, perhaps even refusing to do it. About that time, the boy might begin to have problems at school. He might start experimenting with drugs. The particular forms, though, which his rebellion takes could be many and varied. Regardless of what his son does specifically, the father often views the boy as a "problem," an aggravation (remember, the child occupies the outer circle of interest). Arguments develop between father and son, as each assumes a position and defends it against the other. When the boy wishes his father to be happy (although he may not be capable of thinking all the way through the situation), he pleases his father either by obedience or by accomplishing an outstanding act or deed. When he desires his father angry, he disobeys or does something "bad." The father usually obliges. The child, or rather Satan working through the child, now controls the emotional state of the family rather than the parents. The prevailing emotional state of the family (happiness or anger) depends almost totally upon the behavior of the son. The great preponderance of American families, I believe, are controlled not by the emotional stability of the parents, but by the emotional instability of the children. Thus, families live hurt, frustrated, angry lives and wonder what's wrong with their children.

Parents—Beware!

The responsibility for the child " going wrong," of course, lies squarely upon the shoulders of the father and mother. The emotional attitude of the family should be set by the parents, not the children. When I was a boy, I could not control my mother's emotional state. I might commit a deed worthy of correction, but my mother's emotional appearance never wavered. If I scored five touchdowns in a high school football game (I don't think I ever did), my mother's emotional state never changed. I could not control her. She controlled me. She loved me just as much when I was "bad" as when I was "good.' She was no more proud of me when I was "good" than when I was "bad," at least not outwardly. She was not driven to build me up by becoming elated with my good accomplishments because she never tore me down due to my bad ones. You might question the wisdom in that, for after all the child psychologists maintain that we should brag on our children and build them up when they do well. And we should. However, because we often "put them down" too severely when they are bad, we are sometimes "forced" to build them up abnormally when they are good. Now, I'm not proposing that you and I never tell our children they have done well. We should! Nor am I saying that we should ignore their failings. We should not! Rather, I am maintaining that our children should not be taught that they are only acceptable to us when they do well. They ought not grow up with the idea that their parents love them more when they excel. Our attitudes toward our children ought never to waver, even as the paddle graces our hands. Discipline in love! Spend time solving their problems. That's

God's way. Discipline without love leads to hardness, anger, bitterness. Love without discipline
leads to a lack of respect for authority, permissive-
ness, lack of self-control, insecurity and conflict. A
child who is disciplined and loved and who knows
that both are ever-present will know that he occupies the inner circle of his parents' interest. Therefore he will seldom find himself in control of the
emotional state of the family. Consequently, he will
rarely be an instrument through which Satan might
bring confusion and disunity into the home.

Son I Want You to Bat 500

One other thing needs to be discussed before
leaving this chapter. I believe many parents are
guilty of feeding their own egos with the accomplishments of their children. They want their children to succeed in order to gain attention for
themselves. Childhood athletics and school functions like plays, honors, etc. provide two of the most
apparent places where this attitude might exist.

One summer when I was in college I umpired
little boys' baseball games. Even though it was
twenty-five years ago, I remember like yesterday
the venom and hostility of a mother when I called
her fifteen-year-old son out on strikes. I suddenly
found myself on the receiving end of hysterical
screams of condemnation. Parents, you need to be
very careful when you cheer your children that you
are not pushing them in order to gain personal
pride and satisfaction through their achievements.

May you never put that kind of pressure on young lives, lives capable of being affected by far less pressure. May we never "compete with the Joneses" by using the lives of our children.

Conclusion

With the birth of my grandson, a terrible truth began reverberating in my brain. I found myself, as a grandfather, wanting to do all the things for Brad that I should have done for my children, Fran and Jay. It occured to me that I am not different from many other grandparents. Apparently America is filled with wonderful grandparents. Now, here is the awful truth. Satan is very pleased with that, for God has designed the child to imitate the parent, not the grandparent. We reproduce ourselves in our children, not our grandchildren.

Parents, don't make the mistake that so many of us have already made. As a dear brother in Christ said to me, "The dad should spend some good ol' rock-kicking time with his son and daughter...time spent just enjoying one another with no pressure to get to a meeting or work in the yard, etc." He continued, "A good number of people are teaching these days that it's not the quantity of time you spend with your children, it's the quality of the time." I join with my friend in a hearty, "HOG-WASH!" (whatever that means). How do you determine "quality time"? Whenever a father and a son are enjoying one another's company, that's quality time. Furthermore, ten minutes of that kind of time per week is not enough. Dads, you especially (moms usually enjoy more time with their children than do the fathers) spend a lot of time with those children. Someday, when your priorities have matured a little, you will be glad you did.

God has given to us those precious children, with an explicit set of instructions on how best to rear them. God help us to put our children back into the inner circle of our interests and to tend to their needs at whatever the personal sacrifice.

IX APPLICATION

1 Think back. Do you remember as a child your parents arguing? What was your outward response? What were your inside feelings?

2 Do you argue with your marriage partner in the presence of your children? How do they respond? How do you think it makes them feel?

3 Relate Ephesians 6:4 to your fights with your marriage partner. Can you honestly do both?

4 Men, list the character qualities of your son which came from you. Mothers, do the same thing for your daughters. Why should you then live a Godly life?

5 If your children are grown, do you see anything in their bahavior which reminds you of yourself? List them.

6 In what areas of your children's lives have you overcompensated, or been too lenient? Do you understand how overcompensation tears down boundaries of security?

7 Searching your heart, would you really like for your children to act as adults? If you do feel that way, could it be that as adults, they require less attention and time?

8 Parents, if you had a choice, would you like to be a child again? Why or why not? Are you attempting to look and act younger than you really are?

9 Parents, who really is most important to you in your family, you or your children? Who should be? What ungodly characteristic can be observed in a parent who chooses self over children?

10 Draw the three circles of interest. Now, with no one looking but you and God, place (1) yourself (2) your wife or husband (3) your children (4) your job (5) your leisure time (6) Monday night football (along with Saturday and Sunday) (7) God and other interests and responsibilities in the appropriate circle.

11 Fathers, do you patiently endeavor to develop skills in your son, or do you lack patience with him? Mothers, how about you and your daughter?

12 Now, for a most critical question parents. Who controls the emotional state of your family, you or your children?

13 Parents, won't you commit yourselves to rearing your children as God would have you do it? Why don't you bow your head right now and make that commitment to him!

X

EXCEPT IT BE FOR FORNICATION

When I moved my family to Memphis in 1972 to enroll in Bible College, the divorce rate quoted most often in surveys was one divorce for every four marriages, or twenty-five percent. At this writing, some seven years later, the figure has swelled to more than one out of two, or fifty percent. A mathematician isn't required to decipher that an increase of more than twenty-five percent in seven years roughly equals an average of three and one half percent per year. Various reasons for the increase were discussed earlier. However, one has not been mentioned. We live in an "instant-throw-away" world. We are "blessed" with instant everything from foods to razors. If you want something in a hurry, buy instant and when it gets old or you grow tired of it, discard it and buy another. I wonder if that mentality has crept into marriage. "Let's marry," a couple might plan, "and if the marriage doesn't produce instant bliss, we'll get a divorce." So the divorce rate increases.

As a teacher, preacher and counselor, I face divorce many times in the lives of other people. Its frequency has forced me to search the Scriptures not only for God's law, His "permissive" will (what He allows), but also for His heart, or "perfect" will (what He wants). The results of that search unfold in the following pages.

What Does God Want?

God does have both a permissive and perfect will, you know. Evidences of both are laced throughout Scripture. Perhaps 2 Peter 3:9 presents the clearest indication of His permissive/perfect will. He says, "The Lord is . . . not willing that any should perish, but that all should come to repentance." God (in His heart, or perfect will) wants every person to repent and accept His provision for sin, the Lord Jesus Christ. But do all repent and accept Jesus? Obviously, many do but many, probably more, do not. That leads us to God's permissive will. God's perfect will longs for everyone to become a Christian, but His permissve will allows man a choice. Consequently many reject Him.

The same doctrine holds true in relation to marriage, I believe. God's perfect will desires that none ever divorce for any reason, but Scripture seems to allow it without divine retribution in certain instances. These instances will be examined later in this chapter.

God Hates Divorce

God's perfect will on divorce echoes clearly in Malachi. GOD HATES DIVORCE. May I say that again? GOD HATES DIVORCE! Malachi 2:14-16a says,

> Yet ye say, Wherefore? Because the Lord hath been witness between thee and the wife of thy youth, against whom thou hast dealt treacherously: yet is she thy companion, and the wife of thy covenant. And did not he make one? Yet had he the residue of the spirit. And wherefore one? That he might seek a godly seed. Therefore take heed to your spirit, and let none deal treacherously against the wife of his youth. For the Lord, the God of Israel, saith that he hateth putting away (divorce).
> (parenthesis mine)

The authorized version of this passage might leave us slightly confused due to the seventeenth-century words and phrases. Because of the passage's important nature, however, please examine it rather closely with me.

First, Israel seemed to have questioned God's authority, and that was one of its problems, maybe its foremost problem. The phrase, "Yet ye say, Wherefore?" captures the idea. The Jews apparently exhibited an attitude of, "Oh, come on, God, how have we dealt treacherously and committed an abomination?" (2:11) God informs them that He had witnessed their relationship with their wives, "against whom they had dealt treacherously." God reminds them that from two people, marriage had made them into one. With the residue of the Spirit (the creative power of His Spirit), He could have established the marriage relationship any way that

He had chosen. God elected to make, from the two persons, one flesh, so that the seed, the offspring might be raised in a Godly manner. (Note: There are several other interpretations of this most difficult phrase.) That was God's choice, His design for marriage. But God's way did not please the Jews any more than it satisfies modern America. God made husband and wife into one entity. The husbands deliberately without cause put their wives away, and God hated it. "For the Lord, the God of Israel saith that He hateth putting away." GOD HATES DIVORCE.

Because God hates divorce, Christians should also hate it. I believe I do hate it. I have seen what it can do to a family, to a wife, to children. As chapter one relates, I saw what it did to my family and I have seen it destroy others. Apart from the sovereign work of God in converting the evil which we commit into good (chapter eight), nothing good will ever grow out of a divorce. Our culture's liberal view of divorce ought never to so dull our spiritual sensitivity that we begin to accept it as a viable solution to marital problems. Divorce is not a solution. It is a surrender!

God Does Allow Divorce

However, in both the Old Testament and the New Testament, God allowed divorce under certain conditions. Notice, I said God allowed it. I did not say He encouraged it (although in Ezra He seemed to) nor liked it. In His heart, God hates divorce, but by His law he allows it. "Wait just a minute," you might say. "Doesn't that make God mutable, that is to say, changeable?" Not at all. The relationship between God's perfect will and His permissive will has been taken into account in His way (system) of responding to us. Because of our human frailties and weaknesses, God, in His Grace, allows us to fall short of His perfection. That is precisely why we need a Savior. Jesus carries us to God's perfection by placing His perfection within us. God took human weakness into account when He gave His law in relation to marriage.

Jesus faced the divorce question with the Pharisees. They came to Him one day asking, ". . . is it lawful for a man to put away his wife for every (any) cause?" (parenthesis mine). Following our Lord's monologue in which He restated the account of the creation of male and female and their Godly union as one flesh, the Pharisees countered, "Why did Moses then command to give a bill of divorcement, and to put her away?" Jesus answered, "Moses because of the hardness of your hearts suffered (allowed) you to put away your wives: but from the beginning it was not so" (Matthew 19:3-8, parenthesis mine). Among the several truths which these verses teach, one seems to be that God took into account the people's spiritual condition, thereby allowing divorce in certain situations without condemnation. I believe God continues to do that. Similarly, every time a Christian sins, it is already forgiven in Christ, both instances reflecting God's grace.

Not only did the Old Testament allow divorce in certain situations but in at least two instances it taught that marriage to someone else was acceptable. In the law (Deuteronomy 24:1-2), God through Moses, said, "When a man hath taken a wife, and married her, and it come to pass that she find no favour in his eyes, because he hath found some uncleanness in her: then let him (if he) write her a bill of divorcement, and give it in her hand, and send her out of his house. And when she is departed out of his house, she may go and be another man's wife," (parenthesis mine). Here God clearly allows divorce, in the case of (physical) uncleanness in a woman, and the ensuing marriage of the woman to another man. By implication, God also seems to permit the husband to remarry.

For many conservative Christians, the last chapter of Ezra produces a startling section of Scripture. Cyrus, King of Persia, had been influenced by God to send a group of the dispersed Jews back to Jerusalem to rebuild the temple, which had been destroyed some seventy years before by Nebuchadnezzar, king of Babylon. Following the death of Cyrus, Ezra, a scribe knowledgeable in God's law, requested of a later Persian king that he be allowed to go to Jerusalem in order to ". . . seek the law of the Lord, and to do it, and to teach in Israel statutes and judgments." (Ezra 7:10) Upon arriving in Jerusalem he discovered that many Jewish men had married Gentile women. Some already had children. Ezra, surely under the leadership of God, stood before the people and preached, "Ye have transgressed, and have taken strange wives, to increase the trespass of Israel. Now therefore make confession unto the Lord God of your fathers, and do HIS PLEASURE: and separate yourselves from the people of the land, and from the strange wives." (10:10-11) Verse 16 begins by solemnly declaring, "And the children of the captivity did so . . . ." (emphasis mine).

Perhaps Jeremiah 3:8 provides the most conclusive Scripture teaching the acceptability of divorce in the Old Testament. Here we marvel that God divorced Israel. He will, of course, eventually be wed to the nation again, but that is not the issue. He did divorce His people.

Clearly then, God, in the Old Testament, allowed His people to divorce and to remarry in certain situations without fear of divine chastisement. Notice again now, I said God allowed it. He did not command it, Ezra's order providing possibly the lone exception.

The New Testament

The New Testament appears to teach, not the *desirability* but the *acceptability* of remarriage following a prior marriage, in three situations. In two of the instances the remarriage seems to be allowed following divorce, in the other, after the death of the marriage partner. I said "seems" to be allowed because one of the situations in which remarriage might follow divorce appears relatively clear while the other one is not. Each situation will be examined rather thoroughly.

Several years ago I was awarded the privilege of teaching First Corinthians to an adult Bible class in a Bible College. I taught it again to a Sunday School Class in a rather large church in Memphis. In studying chapter seven the many views of the commentators in regard to divorce and remarriage bothered me somewhat. I determined to discover both God's perfect will and His permissive will in regard to the subject. I suppose my background gave me an added interest in the study, and because the divorce rate continues to increase, God's teaching, I reasoned, becomes increasingly important.

The first truth which I encountered has already been mentioned—"God hates divorce." In any study on the subject, one must continually balance his research with that fact. With that as the basis for the study, I proceeded to search the Scriptures for God's complete will on divorce.

Three Conditions

There seem to be, as already mentioned, three Scriptural conditions whereby a previously married person might remarry. One, fornication, comes from Matthew 19:9. The second one, desertion, is recorded in 1 Corinthians 7:15. First Corinthians 7:39 reveals the third one, death, a seldom-contested doctrine. Of the three, the first two refer to divorce, therefore they will be closely examined.

Matthew 19:9 reads, "And I say unto you,

Whosoever shall put away his wife, except it be for FORNICATION, and shall marry another, committeth adultery: and whoso marrieth her which is put away doth commit adultery." (emphasis mine) Some people interpret this verse of Scripture in "interesting" ways. Perhaps because we want so badly to see Christians live pure lives, to treat marriage partners properly, we often tend to omit from our minds an entire, yet important phrase of that passage, rendering it thusly: "And I say unto you, whosoever shall put away his wife . . . and shall marry another, committeth adultery; and whoso marrieth her which is put away doth commit adultery." The "omitted" phrase reads, ". . . except it be for fornication." May I suggest in love that the "exception clause"ranks just as highly a part of God's Word, just as inspired, as John 3:16. The passage contains an exception clause. Permit me the liberty to write the same message another way by altering the sentence structure. Our Lord seems to be saying that whosoever shall put away his wife *in the case* of fornication and shall marry another *does not* commit adultery. (Notice, I moved the negative but said the same thing.) If a man divorces his wife without her having committed fornication and marries another woman, intercourse with his new wife is adultery. However, if a man divorces his wife because there has been fornication on her part and he marries another, intercourse with his new wife is not adultery. Fornication then becomes an exception clause in the question of divorce and remarriage. When fornication occurs, the innocent party may (not shall, but may) divorce and marry another without committing the sin of adultery.

Some folks insist that Matthew 19:9 refers to the engagement period, often one year, which was customary in the Jewish culture. Therefore, they contend, the verse does not apply to us as written because our marriage customs do not include this period of time, called the espousal period, in which the commitment to marry had been made but the man and woman had not slept together.

In answer to that view, the Scriptures at very best do not seem to support it. In other words, the Bible makes no comment to that effect. The espousal period did in fact exist. However, was a couple married or just engaged during that period? I believe the Word asserts that during the espousal period a couple was actually married. In one well-known verse, Matthew 1:20, the angel appeared to Joseph and said, "Joseph, thou son of David, fear not to take unto thee Mary thy wife . . . ." Joseph was understandably concerned about Mary's pregnancy because they had never "come together" (1:18). Verse 20, quoted above, refers to "Mary, thy wife." They were espoused but she was called his wife. It is possible, even in our culture, for a couple to be married for a while before actually sleeping together. In no way does that reduce their relationship to less than the married state. Apparently it was a common practice in the Jewish culture for the man and woman to live separately for a period of time after they were wed, a period known as the espousal period. Again, in Luke 2:5, Mary is called

Joseph's "espoused WIFE" (emphasis mine). The use of the two words together seems to prove that Mary was Joseph's "wife of the espousal period" as opposed to her being his "wife." In both cases, she was his legal wife. If this interpretation stands, then Matthew 19:9 was written to those who were espoused as well as to those who were actually living together.

Another argument often presented concedes that fornication will break the vows of a marriage as an "exception clause," but fornication is defined as *premarital* intercourse. Therefore, if a man discovered that his wife had engaged in sexual relations with a man before he married her, she bears the guilt of fornication. He then would be free to divorce her, this concept teaches. But can fornication be accurately labeled pre-marital intercourse? The meaning of fornication obviously becomes extremely important.

While studying through the above concept, a shocking thought occurred to me. What if two couples whom we will identify as couple "A" and couple "B," both in their late fifty's, came to me for counsel. Husband "A" says, "I caught my wife in the act of adultery last week with my best friend. It has been going on for several years now. My wife doesn't want me and says she will not stop going to bed with my friend. Does the Bible allow me to divorce her?" According to the popular definition of fornication as pre-marital intercourse, husband "A" may not scripturally divorce his wife because she has committed adultery, not fornication. Adultery is not allowed, according to this view, as a reason to divorce. Couple "B" related a quite different story. Husband "B" relates, "One of my wife's old boyfriends came to visit us last week. He was drunk and blurted out that my wife and he had sex together when they were sixteen years old. My wife then told me that the sex stopped shortly afterward when she accepted Jesus as her Lord and Savior. We married at age twenty-one and have both lived happily together for twenty-nine years, serving the Lord. But I'm afraid that I can't cope with it. Does Scripture allow me the right to divorce my wife?" Because his wife committed fornication, according to the popular view, husband "B" may scripturally divorce his wife and marry someone else, not because of current promiscuity, but because of something which happened thirty-four years ago.

Does that make sense to you? Does that concept reflect the forgiveness of Jesus? If fornication equals pre-marital intercourse, the adulterous wife without repentance and with no intention of stopping cannot be divorced while a Christian wife who has loved and served her husband for many years may be divorced because of a teen-age mistake! I readily confess that this view seems to deny all that the Bible teaches on forgiveness, forgetting, and restitution. So I began a study of the word fornication to determine if it really was pre-marital intercourse.

Fornication—Its Meaning

My first discovery was interesting. I discovered that the original Greek word translated fornication in the New Testament was PORNEIA (a transliteration of the actual Greek word). It does not take much imagination to know that we get the English word "pornography" from it. Using the modern definition (not a conclusive way to determine Biblical meanings, of course), for something to be pornographic does not necessarily indicate intercourse. While the modern definition of a word in no way substitutes as an accurate Biblical interpretation, it will give to us its contemporary meaning. That might then prompt us to study in a given direction. Since the two words pornography and fornication apparently mean the same thing, the contemporary mind should at least wonder if fornication, therefore, might be other sexual acts, in addition to immoral intercourse.

At any rate, my search for the meaning of "porneia" (fornication) led me to research the way the word is used throughout Scripture. In several passages I found the word used in reference to people who almost certainly were married. For example, in Acts 15:20 an entire church, yea, an entire Gentile culture, was commanded to abstain from certain things including fornication. If fornication cannot be committed by those who are married, the command would have been moot, unless of course all the readers were single. Obviously, the Jerusalem Church, which issued the command, desired the churches at Antioch, Syria, and Cilicia to refrain from all sexual impurity, not just illicit intercourse. Likewise, the word fornication was used in reference to entire churches or areas of churches or groups of people in Acts 21:25 (a repeat of the command of Acts 15:20); Romans 1:29; 1 Corinthians 6:18; Ephesians 5:3; Colossians 3:5; and others including Jude 7 and Revelation 9:21. The verb form of the word, "porneuo," appears in Revelation 2:14; 2:20; 17:2; 18:3; and 18:9.

In the Old Testament, the Hebrew words which have been translated fornication are transliterated "taznuth" and "zanah." In 2 Chronicles 21:11, the word "zanah," translated fornication in the King James Bible, likely referred to all the people, both married and single. Ezekiel colorfully accuses the entire nation of Israel of committing spiritual fornication ("taznuth") in 16:15 and 16:29 of the book bearing his name.

When all of these verses are studied together, one thing becomes glaringly clear. Fornication certainly is not restricted to the unmarried. Wives and husbands can commit fornication. Therefore, the word fornication as used in the Scriptures seems to be an "umbrella" term under which all sexual impurity gathers. Fornication might therefore be identified and defined as "all illegal sexual relationships." It would include sexual sins such as adultery, homosexuality, beastiality, sodomy, incest, etc.

Therefore when God declares in Matthew 19:9 that fornication gives an allowable (not desirable) reason for divorce, apparently He is speaking of something which might be "less" than intercourse. In other words, fornication might occur apart from actual intercourse. I have listened to men declare something like this, "I know my wife caught me lying on the couch with her, but we hadn't done anything yet! She doesn't have the right to divorce me!" "My friend," I reply, "you may not admit you have done anything wrong, but according to God's Word you committed fornication." Fornication signifies any illicit sexual relationship. It might occur before intercourse.

Now, lest you misunderstand why God allows divorce because of fornication, let me quickly say that He is not providing an easy exit from a marriage. It's just that God expects and demands absolute purity in a marriage relationship. A husband or wife does not have the "right" to pursue any kind of an illegal, illicit relationship. Husbands, keep your eyes and hands off other women. Wives, stop your sensual dress and lifestyle. God wants absolute purity in your relationship with one another.

Desertion

The second situation in which God, I believe, allows divorce and remarriage in the New Testament emerges from 1 Corinthians 7:15 (the section actually begins in verse 13). Paul writes,

> And the woman which hath an husband that believeth not, and if he be pleased to dwell with her, let her not leave him.

> For the unbelieving husband is sanctified by the wife, and
> the unbelieving wife is sanctified by the husband: else
> were your children unclean; but now they are holy. But if
> the unbelieving depart, let him depart. A brother or a sister
> is NOT UNDER BONDAGE in such cases: but God hath
> called us to peace. (emphasis mine)

So much important information resides in these
verses that it is going to be very difficult discussing
only the issue at hand. The issues under consideration here are the meaning of "not under bondage"
and our Lord's intent in writing these verses. Both
will be probed in depth following one detour into
another area.

I always make a genuine effort to encourage
husbands and wives to stay together, even where
one marriage partner is not a Christian. God wants
them together for several reasons, of course, and
one of them comes from verse 14. The unbeliever is
"sanctified" by the believer. Questions have arisen
concerning the meaning of this powerful word. I
believe Paul uses it here in the same sense that
Ezekiel uses it. Ezekiel 44:19 employs the word
"sanctify" to describe the transmission of holiness
to the people through the garments of the priests, a
forbidden practice. The same concept seems to be
intended in the 1 Corinthians 7 passage, although
the practice there is not a forbidden one. Holiness
flows into the unbeliever and into the family
through the believing partner, regardless of whether the believer is the husband or the wife. Therefore
good counsel would advise the believer to remain
with the unbeliever if for no other reason than to
allow God to have access into the heart of the lost
person.

Not Under Bondage!

Now, before a decision can be reached as to the intent of our Lord in writing these verses, the phrase "not under bondage" ought to be understood. It is a negative statement, as indicated by the word "not." How could we say the same thing positively? "Not under bondage" seems to mean "free." Our Lord records through Paul that when an unbelieving marriage partner leaves, the brother or sister who was left becomes "free." That leads us to another issue.

Obviously "not under bondage" means free, but what is the deserted marriage partner free to do? May she or he stop fulfilling his or her role in the marriage? Might the Christian be free only to divorce without remarrying? Can the deserted partner begin a new lifestyle without seeking a reunion? Is the Christian free to remarry?

To answer these questions, it seems to me that we should examine the setting in which Paul wrote First Corinthians. Obviously, believers in the church at Corinth were, at the very least, considering divorce in order to marry believers. Although the Scriptures fail to express this clearly, from Paul's statements it would probably be safe to assume it to be so. The Christian wife in Corinth likely grew discouraged as she compared her own marriage to a pagan with marriages where both partners were Christians. She must have been tempted to divorce her "old pagan" husband and marry a believer. Paul, though, firmly disallowed it. However he did say that if the unbeliever departed, let him depart. His departure would free the Christian. Since the Corinthian church was not privileged, at the writing of First Corinthians, to have access to the New Testament as we know it, and because no restrictions were applied to that freedom, I believe the Corinthians interpreted "free" as totally free. Therefore, I assume that when the Epistle was read, they understood themselves to be free to function as a single Christian, even to the point of remarrying without fear of Godly reprisal. If God had not intended for them to so conclude, it seems to me that He would have led Paul to include some sort of restriction against the freedom. Since no restrictions were listed, it seems logical to suppose that the Corinthian Christians considered themselves to be totally free, with the freedom to remarry included. Without access to all of the New Testament, their understanding of "not under bondage" most likely would of necessity rest solely upon Paul's letter.

Now, while dogmatism might be appropriate in relation to the exception clause of Matthew 19:9, it probably is not appropriate in relation to 1 Corinthians 7:15. Someday, when I face my Lord, I may discover that I erred in my interpretation of this part of Paul's epistle. I may discover that I am wrong prior to facing my Lord. Even now I am willing to listen to other interpretations of the passage. In the meantime, I have no choice but to continue interpreting the passage as written above, i.e., that desertion gives an allowable, although not desirable, condition for divorce and remarriage.

Finally, two other questions ought to be examined: What happens when a believer leaves a believer? and, When does departure become desertion? My answers, and may I emphasize that these are *my* answers, not Scripture's, are: first, that the emphasis of the passage points to desertion, not whether the deserter is a Christian. The particular situation in Corinth included Christians married to non-Christians. However, the passage really seems to teach that in the case of desertion, the deserted party may remarry. A great deal of question persists in my mind, personally, that a genuine Christian would desert his or her family. Not many professing Christians whom I have known have done it.

The second question, "When does departure become desertion," remains specifically unanswered in the Bible. Since God gave no exact instructions, I believe that a safe definition of desertion would be, "When a person, male or female, leaves his or her family and establishes another residence away from his or her family expressly for the purpose of no longer functioning as a member of the family." Now, because the Word of God does not indicate an exact meaning of desertion, I realize, and yield to the possibility, that my definition might be far from God's thinking. Because our Lord did not define the concept for us, I have endeavored to create a definition. In counseling, the counselor needs to work in clear, definite directions. I believe that our Lord permits each culture and generation to examine its lifestyle and institute, from that examination, a concept of desertion. (Note: Apparently He has done the same thing in wedding ceremonies, for He has not instructed the church on how to conduct one.) I believe that the above definition of desertion does not offend Jesus nor does it deny Scripture, while at the same time it describes the act in relation to our fluid, mobile society. Before we leave the subject of desertion, however, please understand that I am *not* encouraging a deserted marriage partner to divorce the deserter and to marry someone else. Quite the contrary. Obviously, because some questions remain unanswered, not only about the meaning of desertion, but also whether desertion permits a person to divorce and to remarry, extreme caution ought to be taken by the deserted partner. He or she may want to wait until the deserter brings up the subject of divorce before considering it. It would not be ungodly for the deserted partner to wait until the deserter remarries before considering remarriage, although Scripture does not seem to require it. God can, and has, put together again what man has torn asunder. My counsel always gives God an opportunity to put the marriage back together.

The third instance in which marriage to a second marriage partner may occur involves death. Since little confusion surrounds this teaching, little space will be attributed to it. The Scriptural reference should be mentioned though, along with one comment. First Corinthians 7:39 declares, "The wife is bound by the law as long as her husband liveth; but if her husband be dead, she is at liberty to be married to whom she will; only in the Lord."

The first phrase of that passage, "The wife is bound by the law as long as her husband liveth . . ." should be read in context. As already established, two Scriptural exceptions to the phrase seem to exist. Apart from these two conditions, the wife and apparently the husband are bound to the marriage for life.

Conclusion

In conclusion to this most important issue, one word of caution ought to be considered. Those of us who teach the Word of God would do well to make as certain as we possibly can that we are not guilty of imposing the same thing upon our people as the Scribes and Pharisees did in Jesus' day. Matthew 23:1-4 states,

> Then spake Jesus to the multitude, and to his disciples, Saying, The Scribes and the Pharisees sit in Moses' seat: All therefore whatsoever they bid you observe, that observe and do; but do not ye after their works: for they say, and do not. For they bind heavy burdens and grievous to be borne, and lay them on men's shoulders; but they themselves will not move them with one of their fingers.

Apparently, the Scribes and Pharisees increased the laws under which God's people labored. Through time and tradition they had expanded God's law to suit their own whims and fancies. This burden upon the people lodged unapproved by God. Jesus referred to those who imposed their own views upon others as hypocrites. God will ". . . lay upon you no greater burden than these necessary things." (Acts 15:28) Let us be very careful not to superimpose our beliefs and ideas about divorce and remarriage over the printed words of the Scriptures. To impose guilt upon a person who has not broken the Law of God is a heinous sin in itself.

GOD HATES DIVORCE! But I believe the entire Bible will bear me out when I say that he hates fornication more than he hates divorce.

X APPLICATION

1 With your Bible and a complete concordance, look up and list all passages which include the word fornication. How many times is the word obviously used in relation to an entire church?

2 Write out in your own words the definition of fornication which you might have had before reading this chapter. Compare that definition with the result of your research in question 1.

3 Examine your own concept of divorce and remarriage. Upon what is that concept based? What does Scripture say about it?

4 What often establishes a person's view of divorce and remarriage, Scripture, tradition, or the cultures in which he lives? What should determine it?

5 Since God hates divorce, do you? Should you? Should you hate the divorcee?

6 Would you agree that legalism might be defined as "being dogmatic about that which the Bible isn't . . ."? Have you ever been tempted to be a legalist?

7 Since God hates divorce, why don't you commit yourself to never being a part of it? Will you do that right now?

XI

GOD'S PORTRAIT OF A GODLY MARRIAGE

The Bible features several sections of Scripture which direct God's children toward Godly marital relationships. Not the least of these are Ephesians 5:21-33 and Colossians 3:18-19. However, as a counselor, the passage to which I find myself turning most often is 1 Peter 3:1-7. It reads:

> Likewise, ye wives, be in subjection to your own husbands; that, if any obey not the word (Word), they also may without the (a) word be won by the conversation (conduct) of the wives; While they behold your chaste (pure) conversation (conduct) coupled with fear. Whose adorning let it not be that outward adorning of plaiting the hair, and of wearing of gold, or of putting on of apparel; But let it be the hidden man of the heart, in that which is not corruptible, even the ornament of a meek and quiet spirit, which is in the sight of God of great price. For after this manner in the old time the holy women also, who trusted in God, adorned themselves, being in subjection unto their own husbands: Even as Sara obeyed Abraham, calling him lord: whose daughters ye are, as long as ye do well, and are not afraid with any amazement. Likewise, ye husbands, dwell with them according to knowledge, giving honour unto the wife, as unto the weaker vessel, and as being heirs together of the grace of life; that your prayers be not hindered. (Parenthesis mine)

A Godly Wife

What is submission? Hopefully, chapter five answered that question for you. Therefore, because of our previous examination of submission, I will not delve very deeply into it again. However, let me remind the wives that when God commands you to submit to your husbands, He is referring to "what you do" as opposed to "who you are." Two basic teachings demand the making of that distinction. First the American culture sometimes denies the concept of submission altogether. Over against that, some Christians teach that wives must submit even their intellects, emotions and wills to their husbands. We have shown, I believe, both to be non-scriptural teachings.

Once Biblical submission is understood, its importance cannot be overly stressed. Perhaps for that reason God introduced 1 Peter 3 with the doctrine. All wives inherit the command, but those who are married to unbelievers are especially counseled to submit. (That is a "far cry" from much Christian counseling, so called, which teaches just the opposite.) The passage itself contains the reason. Christian wives ought to submit to unsaved husbands in order that their husbands might be won to the Lord. The language of the authorized or King James Version Bible might not be comprehensible to twentieth-century Americans, however. Therefore we should examine the verse carefully. (You may have noticed, in the recording of the entire passage on the first page of this

chapter, that I included additional words in parenthesis for clarity.)

A Witness From Your Life

First, God teaches you, ladies, that you should
submit to your unsaved husbands because they
have rejected the Word of God. They have not
obeyed the Word (notice the capital "W," which
ought to be there), that is, they have not received a
witness from the Word. Don't, in addition, deprive
them of receiving a witness from your life! Unfortunately, some Christian wives who are married to
unconverted husbands wallow in self-pity because
of their plight and even envy other women who
have Christian husbands. They thereby deprive
themselves of being used to minister to their
husbands. Occasionally God grants to me the privilege of seeing a wife commit her life to be so used. A
more powerful testimony does not exist. A man who
mistreats his wife, and yet receives love in return,
often faces the ire of even his non-Christian friends.
To that, add his inability to transfer guilt to his wife
(because of her loving response to him) and the
product is a miserable man, primed, hopefully, for
receiving the gospel. A living testimony bears itself
in silence. It doesn't require a word from a wife.
God conveys it through the wife's conduct. (A
reminder about the word "conversation" should be
given. The original word would best be translated
"conduct," perhaps including talk but not majoring
upon it. That the word would best be translated

"conduct" springs from the passage itself. How could someone be won by conversation without a word? See Chapter Four.)

Verse two expands upon the message of verse one, explaining that the lost husband ought to see, in the behavior of his wife, "chaste conduct" and "fear." Both will be examined very carefully.

Chastity and Respect

Christian woman, are you married to an unsaved man? Does he see in you chaste, that is, pure behavior? Do you have eyes only for him? Or does he have reason to question your faithfulness? Your conduct ought to rise above reproach as you display the Lord Jesus Christ to your husband. Love him when he is unlovable, as Christ did you. The more distant he seems, the more committed to him you ought to become. You may be God's only instrument through which he can see Jesus, especially if he has rejected the church. See yourself as a minister of the gospel; a minister to one person; a minister without pride, for it is the one characteristic which must be discarded in order for you to respond to your husband scripturally.

Christian wife, God continues, to chaste behavior, add fear. You are certainly aware, however, that God is not commanding you to fear for your safety. Nor does He demand that your life be characterized by fear, according to the contemporary definition of the word. For after all, "Perfect love casteth out all (of that kind of) fear." God does seem to be admonishing you, though, to "respect" your husband. Don't struggle against his occupancy of the office of "captain" of the ship of marriage, whether or not he has been redeemed.

"Godly" Does Not Equal Sensual

Verse three forbids you, Christian wife, to appeal to your husband on the basis of the physical. Of all the ignored verses of Scripture in the Bible, 1 Peter 3:3 might lead the group. Because it is often disregarded, and because of its importance, permit me to requote it. "Whose adorning let it NOT BE THAT OUTWARD adorning of plaiting the hair, and of wearing of gold, or of putting on of apparel . . . ." (caps mine).

Satan has done a masterful job of sensualizing women. Notice, I did not say feminizing. I said sensualizing. There is a marked and Satanic difference. God does not require Christian women to be the sleek, sulky, sensual creatures Hollywood has for too long depicted them to be. Forgive me if I start preaching (although preaching is the highest profession of man), but "my blood stirs" a little when I think of Hollywood's influence upon God's fairer creation. A wife who has lost her figure (through childbirth or age or for some other reason) often seems to be viewed as one of the world's misfits. Husbands have even used that flimsy excuse for committing adultery. After all, the world teaches, an overweight woman cannot be sensual. Therefore, it maintains, she cannot be a good wife, nor even a positive influence in society. Why, apparently even American business cannot function without sensual-looking women "pushing" its products. From automobiles to shaving cream, marketing supposedly requires sensuality. Where, pray tell, does the Word of God suggest that? You and I both know, in our honest moments, that Satan, not God, authors it. Why then do Christian women get pulled into that kind of lifestyle! Ladies, there is nothing immoral nor unfeminine about sweat and muscles and calluses on your hands, in spite of Hollywood's message. As a matter of fact, a careful reading of Proverbs 31:10-31 reveals that God's woman "... worketh willingly with her hands (13b); "... girdeth her loins with strength, and strengtheneth her arms" (17); and "... layeth her hands to the spindle, and her hands hold the distaff" (19). Those characteristics, and the others listed there, feature women who are known by their "strength and honor." What a contrast to the "perfect woman" seen every day on television. I listen to the results of Satan's ungodly concept of femininity from husbands all the time; "She doesn't excite me any more," they moan. These men are really saying that they don't lust after their wives any more because they (the wives) don't measure up to Hollywood's (really Satan's) standard of sensuality.

Along with all its heinous results, one good thing has burst forth from the Women's Liberation Movement. The leaders of the movement, misguided and blind though they seem to be, are doing something which Christians and the church should have done long ago but for the most part have not done. Women's Lib warns that women will no longer assume the role of "sex object." May God forgive us for forcing our wives and daughters into the mold of sex object in the first place. May He break our hearts until we view them as our Lord does.

God clearly reinforces 1 Peter 3:3 in 1 Timothy 2:9. "... Women adorn themselves in modest apparel, with shamefacedness (modesty) and sobriety; not with braided hair, or gold, or pearls, or costly array...." (parenthesis mine). Because man can be tempted through his eyes and because he usually possesses the intense sexual drive, women ought to dress and deport themselves modestly. Satan, on the other hand, tempts women to act and to exhibit their bodies in a sensual manner (thus increasing the sexual urge in men), while at the time cautioning men to "look the other way" if they wish not to lust. Whether these ungodly women realize it or not (most do, I believe), the knowledge that men are lusting after them feeds their starving egos. Of course, by assuming that position, women disclaim any responsibility for engendering lust in men. Certainly, before God, men must bear their own guilt for lust, but because God apparently cautions women against sensuality, they too must stand guilty before Him.

To Whom are You Listening?

Just as surely as 1 Peter 3:3 tells a woman how *not* to appeal to her husband, verse four explains how she *ought* to respond to him. "But let it be the hidden man of the heart, in that which is not corruptible, even the ornament of a meek and quiet spirit, which is in the sight of God of great price." Ladies, although at first it may not be apparent, God offers you protection in this verse. If you appeal to your husband on the basis of the outward, the physical, the sensual, you probably will not win the ongoing battle against "time." You are growing older. A day will come when the natural aging process will strip from you a portion of your physical beauty. If through the years you have appealed to your husband on the basis of the external, thereby encouraging and developing in him a response to sensuality, don't be shocked when, after age has sapped yours, you find him responding to younger, more sensual women. Many eighteen-year-old women are willing to go out with thirty-year-old men. There are many twenty-eight-year-old women who will date forty-year-old men. There are many thirty-five-year-old women willing to see fifty-year-old men. I write from experience. I counsel abandoned wives almost every day. From my testimony you will remember that I too was guilty of abandoning mine. Probably ninety-five percent of the abandoned wives have been left for younger, more sensual-looking and acting women. Look around you. Isn't that true?

Lady, God reminds you to appeal to your husband on the basis, not of the outward person, for that will go away, but on the basis of the "inward man." Appeal to your husband on the basis of the incorruptible things, i.e., a meek and quiet spirit. God places great value on these two things. Wives, the question is, "To whom are you listening? To God or to the world and Satan?"

And All In The Name of Jesus!

Before I explain "meek" and "quiet," two often-misunderstood words, please let me digress for a moment. In recent years many so-called Christian books have been published by "Christian" authors who promote the idea that a wife should appeal to her husband through the "God-given tools of sex and sensuality." The wedding bed cannot be defiled, they teach, misinterpreting Hebrews 13:4. In other words, whatever happens in the bedroom between husband and wife is acceptable! Apparently no scriptural evidence exists to prove that theory, however. Consuming lust is a sin regardless of whom the object of the lust might be. Sex was given by God, first, for the propagation of the race. Secondly, through the proper use of it, the man and woman are illustrating how they become "one flesh." There doesn't seem to be any Scripture allowing, authorizing, condoning, or even suggesting the acceptability of any sex act other than normal intercourse, and that between husband and wife. The Christian's life must harbor no sensuality, 1 Peter 3:3-4 clearly teaches. These two verses alone still the voices of many of the so-called Christian authors today. However, they are not the only two verses which cry out against sensuality.

The Bible, it appears, identifies sensuality and lust as sins. It does not, contrary to what I am often told by counselees, seem to distinguish between sensuality in a wife; lust toward one's wife; and general sensuality and lust. As a matter of fact, I'm not certain that a man can direct his lust toward his wife only. A man's wife may provide relief for his lust, but she may not necessarily be the object of it. Since the Bible does not differentiate between "lust for a wife" and "lust generally," all lust must be labeled sin. If, however, lust leads to an immoral relationship, fornication, an additional sin, occurs.

Abnormal Sexual Acts

One of the marks of sensuality is an almost uncontrollable urge to commit abnormal sexual acts. Paul speaks in Ephesians 4:19 of those consumed by it when he writes, "Who being past feeling (emotion) have given themselves over unto lasciviousness, to work all uncleanness with greediness." The Old English word lasciviousness could properly be translated "sensuality." Notice the characteristics of people caught in the trap of sensuality. They have descended beyond "feeling," or emotional concern for others. It matters little that their wives (or in some cases their husbands) want to be spared from participating in a certain sexual activity. Those enslaved to sensuality have become callous to the welfare of others, and particularly to their mate's sexual wishes. Secondly, they find themselves at the mercy of their own lusts, which permeate every area of their lives and influence their every decision. Sensuality owns them. They are its slave. Thirdly, they want to taste it all, to work all uncleanness. They usually leave no perverted act untried. Fourthly, they grow greedy for it. A greedy person wants everything for himself. Selfishness identifies the sensual person. He can usually be spotted reading Playboy, Penthouse or other pornographic literature. The words ". . .given themselves over . . . ." suggests that fact. A lusting person possesses a ravenous appetite for sex and he often attempts to feed it through pornographic literature, which does not work, of course. Rather than satisfying lust, pornographic literature increases it. Another mark of the sensual person is a dissatisfaction with normal intercourse. As a matter of fact, intercourse provides a good way to distinguish illicit lust from normal God-given sexual desire. If marital intercourse satisfies sexual desire, then the sex drive can probably be labeled "Godly." If, however, intercourse does not satisfy, then that desire has probably exceeded God's boundaries. It is likely lust.

I will end the digression with one clarification. In discussing sensuality, I am not degrading normal and proper hygiene. God places a lot of importance upon purification, both ceremonial and physical.

Back to "Meek"

Now back to "meek." Somehow, perhaps because the words "sound" similar, we seem to assign the definition of "weak" to the word "meek," an obvious mistake. Meek has been properly defined as "strength under control." Weak depicts little strength and little or no emotional control. Ladies, when God charges you to exhibit a meek and quiet spirit, He is directing you toward inward beauty. He wants you to influence your wayward husband His way: that is, through strength; through emotional and verbal control; and with a quiet spirit. Now, in contrast to what the world says, that is God's picture of a Godly woman. When you so respond to your husband, he cannot reasonably transfer his guilt, which comes from his misconduct, to you. He must bear its burden himself, a necessary step in bringing him to God. Whether or not, however, your husband ever acknowledges or responds to your meek and quiet spirit, you know that the Owner of your soul does. Why not do it for Him? Jesus said, "Why callest thou me Lord, Lord and do not the things which I say?"

Like all good preachers, Peter illustrates his message with people. In verses 5 and 6, he ends the address to women by saying, ". . . and are not afraid with any amazement." The New American Standard Bible states it, ". . . without being frightened by any fear." Ladies, you ought to suffer no fear if you obey God. "Oh," you might be tempted to say, "if I begin to appeal to my husband this way now, he might grow tired of me," or "He might not like it," or "It might not work, I might lose him." Have no fear, God says. If obeying God causes your husband to leave, then so be it. He would have left anyway, else

God would not have told you to have no fear. Have you deposited your husband into the safekeeping hands of God? That is the issue.

A Wise Husband

Although God addresses only one verse, 1 Peter 3:7, to the man, that one verse is "loaded." If husbands understood and obeyed only 1 Peter 3:7 there would be a notable decrease in the divorce rate, not to mention a decline in marital misery.

"Likewise, ye husbands, dwell with them (wives) according to knowledge . . . ." God commands all husbands to know their wives and to know how to dwell, or live, with them. Some of you might exclaim, "How do you do that? I've lived with her twenty years and I still haven't figured her out!" Well, you need to start trying. God commands it.

How then do you dwell with your wife according to knowledge? Apparently, 1 Peter informs husbands that women usually respond, act, and react to situations differently. Fellows, we need to understand that fact and adjust our lives to it, rather than fuming over it and condemning it. God created a difference in women, as you and I readily recognize. He then commanded us, men, to adjust our lives to our wives, compensating for that difference.

Emotional make-up supplies one easily-visible difference between most men and women. Women possess more sensitivity, normally, than men. Most men can joke with one another and call one another descriptive names like "fatso" without offense. But, fellows, that is not so with your wives. They are much more sensitive than we. While men might laugh and return one another's jokes, wives often turn on the tears. That fact could not have been illustrated more clearly than it was several years ago with my wife, Foy, and daughter, Fran.

To tell the story, I'm forced to tell you a little about myself. I know almost nothing about "matching" clothes, although at one time I thought I did. At the time of the lesson with Foy and Fran, I served on the staff of a Bible College. Foy, Fran, my son, Jay, and I had gotten up early, as usual, for our family devotions around the breakfast table. After finishing, I went back into our bedroom to dress for work. Our house was designed so that anyone standing at the kitchen sink could look through the den, down the hallway to our bedroom door. Foy and Fran were standing at the sink washing breakfast dishes when I came out of the bedroom. I was superbly (I thought) clothed. I had on beautiful stripes. I wore a striped sport coat and striped trousers, with a striped shirt and a beautiful striped tie. Even though the stripes were a little different, I thought I had done a fine job that day of matching the colors. When I entered the den where Fran and Foy could see me, however, in unison they exclaimed, "You're not going to wear THAT are you?" I stopped dead in my tracks, foiled again. One of the bright spots in my day comes when I safely slip out of the house without being inspected. History has taught me that an inspection usually brings a change in some part of my clothing. (The most logical location for my clothes closet is at the door which opens to our garage. That's where I usually change clothes.)

My second mistake (my first was my mis-match) was my reply to Foy and Fran. "I'm not going to the Mid-South Bible College fashion show!" Everything grew very quiet. I walked on into the kitchen, glancing left, to where Foy and Fran were standing at the sink. Tears! Streaming down Foy's cheeks were great big tears. I couldn't see Fran clearly because she was standing on the other side of Foy, but it looked like her condition was about the same as her mother's. I looked to my right, to where Jay sat at the table. His hands were cupped over his mouth. With all of his might he was hopelessly attempting to suppress a laugh. Astounding! The very same words which had hurt my ladies, drew laughter from my son. Why? Because women are more sensitive than men! Men, God expects us to recognize our wives' sensitivity, that is, to dwell with them "according to knowledge."

A Precious Vessel

The second command of verse 7 reads, ". . . giving honour unto the wife, as unto the weaker vessel . . . ." Which word in that phrase seems more important to you? Did the word "weaker" first gain your attention? If it did, you are probably a man. If you are a woman, though, your eyes probably focused upon the word "honour." Ladies, I believe you are right. "Honour" seems to be the primary word. Is God teaching, though, that we men are to honor our wives because they are weak? If you think so, why would God command you to honor weakness? A Christian wife has received "not the spirit of fear; but of power, and of love, and of a sound mind," (2 Timothy 1:7) all of which denote strength, not weakness. Or to ask the question another way, are Christian wives expected to be weak, even though many passages of Scripture teach all believers to be strong in the Lord (Romans 5:6; Proverbs 31:10-31; Psalm 24:8; Romans 15:;1, etc.)? The obvious answer is "No." God cannot teach a concept contrary to other Scripture. God never places a spiritual premium upon weakness, feminine or otherwise. (He allows us to become weak so He can strengthen us, 2 Corinthians 12:9-10.) A Christian wife, like her husband, ought to be strong in the Lord's strength. Why then does God command men to "give honour unto their wives as unto the weaker vessel?" It seems to me that men are to honor their wives like a "more fragile" vessel, or dish, is valued. God is not describing the wife as a vessel, weaker or otherwise, although her body may be a vessel of the Holy Spirit. That concept, however, is not being discussed here. On the other hand, God seems to be saying that men should honor their wives like they might honor very fragile dinnerware. Now, my ignorance of clothes is surpassed only by my ignorance of china, but I take this phrase to mean that I ought to honor my wife like I would honor very fragile, thus very expensive, pieces of china. In spite of my ignorance, I'm conscious of the fact that my wife handles some dishes with greater care than others. She often leaves the "every day" dinnerware stacked in the sink, later to be deposited in the dishwasher. No one would insist that she bestow honor upon these vessels. However, when the occasion so demands, Foy uses her better china, which she handles more delicately. With great care, she usually washes each piece gently by hand and immediately places it back in its proper storage space. She honors it because it is more fragile, more expensive, more precious. Men, God expects us to honor our wives that very same way, as though they were precious vessels.

Please forgive me for using so many personal illustrations, but a family situation occured which provides just that, a perfect illustration of how we men are to honor our wives as "precious." Because of the divorce and all of its anguish, my daughter Fran was immeasurably hurt. So was my son, Jay, but not being as old as Fran, he was not damaged as greatly. When Foy and I were saved, even before we were remarried, Fran and Jay and I sat down on the patio steps of our home and I said again, as I had many times before, that "Mommie and I are going back together and this time we're going to make it." Of course Fran, who was only ten years old at the time, and Jay, who was eight, had no way of knowing that Jesus could make that much difference in a marriage. Furthermore, because they had never known real love; because they had been born and reared in the midst of drunken parties, hate, fighting and bitterness; because they feared more failure and pain; they probably did not want us to fail again. Anyway, it made little difference to them that we were going to "give it another try." For seven and one half years after Foy and I remarried, Fran still had not accepted me. As a matter of fact, when I attempted to hug her, she would physically pull away. Her disgust for me was written in her face. But through circumstances and God's abundant grace, she came back to me. Today, no father on earth has a more loving daughter.

But now, for the illustration! On Christmas Day, 1977, I unwrapped a present from Fran, a coffee mug. Across one side of it were three of the most beautiful words these eyes have ever seen—-WORLD'S GREATEST DAD! For a few days I drank from it at home. I realized, however, that my mug was not as precious to other members of my family as it was to me, when I noticed it teetering precariously high atop a stack of dirty dishes. Retrieving it from the "jaws of death," I carried it to my office where I meet most of my counseling sessions. I don't drink coffee out of it any more. As a matter of fact, that precious vessel rests upon the top of my book shelf, in a place of prominence. I put it there, not only for protection, but also as a visible illustration of 1 Peter 3:7. Few men counselees come into my office who aren't told the story. You see, that coffee mug is a precious vessel to me. I handle it with great care. Husbands, I believe God would have you honor your wives that way. You should place upon them great value, as you would a precious vessel.

HEIRS TOGETHER

"... And as being heirs together of the grace of life...." With these words God teaches husbands a profound truth. We are not *superior* heirs of the grace of life, neither are we *inferior* heirs, but rather *co-heirs* of the grace of life with our wives. Through eternity, men, we will enjoy the presence of our Christian wives, not as wives, but as sisters. They are co-heirs with us of eternal life. The one with whom we have shared an intimate lifetime, who knows us as we really live in the seclusion of our homes, will be in Heaven with us. That means that two people in Heaven will know the innermost secrets of our hearts, Jesus and our wives. God mercifully reminds us that we will face them eternally as a sister. No marital chain of command will exist in Heaven. Everyone will be equal apart from the natural separation between the Creator and the created. Men, we would be wise therefore to honor our wives now, so that we will not face them in guilt eternally.

The Clincher

And now, for the clincher! Men, God simply, yet directly, reminds us of the consequence of disobedience in three areas, i.e., seeking to understand your wives; giving honor to them; and recognizing them as co-heirs of the grace of life. Our prayers will be hindered.

Upon teaching this verse to a group of men in a seminar awhile back, I concluded, "Therefore, men, if your prayers aren't rising past the ceiling, if God isn't hearing them, it could indicate that you are disobeying God in one or more of these areas. God will not answer your prayers." One of the men took great issue with me. He insisted that the verse doesn't say that God would refuse to hear our prayers, but rather that our prayers would only be hindered, or only affected. The fellow may be right, of course. To hinder probably doesn't strictly mean to stop altogether. But the verse does declare that the prayers of a guilty man will be extremely affected. The verse probably teaches, in context, that God might choose to ignore the prayers of a husband who violates these precepts. At the very least, his prayers would be adversely influenced. Few of us can afford to have our feeble prayer life affected to any degree. Obviously God, in 1 Peter 3:7, intends to reveal the importance of proper attitudes and actions toward our wives, as well as chastening's severity when we disobey.

CONCLUSION

Husbands, I dare say that few women exist who would not commit their lives completely to husbands who live by 1 Peter 3:7. When that verse combines with the command of Ephesians 5:25 which says, "Husbands, love your wives even as Christ also loved the church, and gave Himself for it," foolish indeed would be an unresponding woman.

XI APPLICATION

1 Do you agree with the writer about the concept of submission? Why or why not? How would you explain it?

2 Ladies, do you find submission to your husband to be difficult? Why or why not?

3 Men, do you seem to have trouble submitting to your employer? To the government? Why or why not?

4 Does your life witness to the lost? Ladies, does your life witness to your husband?

5 Wives, are you careful never to cause your husband to doubt your loyalty to him? Has he ever accused you? Did he have a reason?

6 Ladies, have you read any books lately which suggested that you should appeal to your husband sensually? Did the book provide any Scripture to prove its point? Are you aware of any?

7 Ladies, are you really confident that you can retain your husband's attention if you respond to him according to 1 Peter 3:4? Why don't you commit yourself to obeying God according to 1 Peter 3:1-6 right now.

8 What effect do you think the sensual T.V. programs are having upon people today? What might the programs be causing in children?

9 Husbands, list the obvious emotional and mental differences between you and your wife? Have you made a real effort to understand that difference? Why don't you make a commitment to that effect now?

10 Husband, just how precious to you is your wife? Do you honor your wife? Look the word "honor" up in a dictionary. Now, do you honor her? What are some ways this "honor" will be expressed?

11 Finally, husbands and wives, why not commit yourselves right now never to deal treacherously with one another; to respond

to each other according to the Word, not the flesh (under the influence of pride); and to be all that God would have you be both in the home and out of it?

XII

CONCLUSION

God hates divorce! God gives His Spirit to those who receive His Son as Lord and Savior! God's Spirit has power!

With those words, we conclude that God can change men and women. God can heal hurts, and He can enable His own to take a great deal of abuse, even from those whom they love most, husbands and wives. But God changes and strengthens only through obedience to Him.

God converts problems and evil into good. For a Christian, therefore, the problem is never the problem. The problem is always the Christian's response to the problem. Once God's child determines to obey his Lord and does it, God guarantees to convert the problem into good.

May God gain control over our hearts and minds so that His will can become our own and His way the goal of our lives.